Th
Hu
Cooking

PAULA POGANY BENNETT
& VELMA R. CLARK

Drawings by
Willy Pogany

HIPPOCRENE BOOKS
New York

Acknowledgments

Our gratitude goes to those friends who so graciously and generously contributed their help.

Our special thanks to Mrs. Marie Menlo for her invaluable suggestions and unflagging interest and encouragement.

To Miss Sophie Wilds for her ever-willing counsel.

To Mrs. Klara Roman and Mrs. Kata Halász for putting at our disposal old Hungarian recipes.

To Mrs. Elaine Pogany for her excellent advice as a famous hostess of Hungarian cooking in America.

And to Mrs. Margaret Anthony, Mrs. Enid Botsford and Mrs. Tanya Toombs for following the recipes and proving that Hungarian cooking can be done with glorious results here in America.

A warm acknowledgment goes to Mrs. Julia Bencze Dull, Mrs. Ilonka Dragos and Miss Anna Kiss for contribution of their native Székely (Transylvanian) dishes which they transplanted in true form to America, their new country.

And to Mrs. Helen Hovey, who originated and encouraged the idea of writing this book, we express our deepest gratitude.

The Authors

Hippocrene paperback edition, 1993.

Revised edition, 1997.

For information, address:
HIPPOCRENE BOOKS, INC.
171 Madison Avenue
New York, NY 10016

ISBN 0-7818-0586-4

Printed in the United States of America.

Contents

Preface

Songs of Hungary reveal that love and food are closely entwined in the hearts of this frankly and enthusiastically food-loving nation. The zest for good food and fine wines is expressed not only in poetry but in folk songs gaily recited or sung on convivial occasions. Many a fiery *csárdás* is danced to songs and music in which the words are of food and cooking.

Good Hungarian cooking is a delightful accomplishment. In Hungary the spirit with which a special dish is cooked is almost as important as the ingredients and the measurements.

I believe, too, that Hungarian cooking is a fine art and, as such, has an emotional appeal. I even suggest that one who is unfamiliar with Hungarian background might turn on the radio and listen to Hungarian folk music played by gypsies, or perhaps to recordings of such music, as she cooks.

Hungarian cooking is not spicy. It is pleasing in a sophisticated way, having that indefinable quality which also distinguishes the people.

In this book there are many varieties of menus to be found—dishes to bring adventure to your cooking, give satisfaction to you as cook and hostess over and above the pleasure and enjoyment these dishes will afford your family and guests.

Paula Pogany Bennett

HUNGARIAN FOODS AND MENUS

HUNGARIAN FOODS AND MENUS

Hungarian food enjoys a popularity all its own. It is as well known—and nearly as colorful—as the picturesque folk costumes of old Hungary, as unforgettable as the country's gypsy music. The people have a marked appreciation of good food, and the housewife spares neither time nor effort to achieve perfection. She considers her cooking a labor of love. Through food she most naturally expresses the generous hospitality characteristic of Hungarian country folk. It is not unusual for a feast to be enthusiastically spread even at great sacrifice to the family.

This prominence of food and the Hungarian flair for making it good are not surprising since Hungary is a country rich in products of the soil. The "Great Plain" is one of the world's most fertile basin areas, where both rain and sunshine are abundant. From its grain fields, its meadows and orchards, and its celebrated vineyards, superior foods are grown. Vast pastures, where great herds of long-horned cattle graze, produce the finest meat, milk, butter, and cheese. Hardy gray-black sheep, roaming the hills, furnish both mutton and wool, and on every farm pigs are fattened. Lake Balaton and the Danube and Tisza rivers offer their bounty of fish, an important and favorite food. This plenty, this inexhaustible reservoir of natural resources, has made the Hungarian a lavish cook.

The food pattern of Hungary has developed with its history. As in America, many peoples and religions have merged, and the country has been enriched in the process. Slovaks, Serbs, Croats, Poles, Slovenes, Russians, Rumanians, and Germans, all have contributed to the Magyar kitchen. Probably the greatest, certainly the longest-lasting, influence was that of the Turks, who dominated Hungary for one hundred and fifty years. Coffee, melons, tropical fruits, nuts, spices, and seasonings were introduced by the conquering pashas.

Royal marriages also caused significant changes in food habits. The Italian Queen Beatrix and the French Queen Anne brought a greater delicacy to the cuisine of the Hungarian court. This was a happy influence. Rich, heavily spiced dishes lost none of their native characteristics while they were freed of certain of their cruder qualities. The discreet use of garlic became known; butter was preferred to the use of lard; and sometimes sweet cream replaced the familiar sour variety.

But with all the foreign influence, Hungarian food has retained much of its originality. Contributions from the outside only added variety and refinement. Most important of these was the introduction of paprika. It is generally conceded that paprika "invaded the country" with the Turkish conquest of the fifteenth century and since then has given national character to the food. At first paprika was considered a lowly spice, dear to the peasant who could not afford precious imported spices. Gradually its use spread in a rather clandestine manner through the kitchens to the tables of the nobility. Today no Hungarian kitchen would be without a liberal supply of native-grown paprika—bright red and finely ground. Good Hungarian cooking requires it. It is generously used in many dishes and supersedes all other seasonings.

Hungarian paprika, fondly described as "*nemes édes* [noble and sweet]," has an indescribably richer flavor than Spanish or American paprika. This is due to the alluvial soil in which it thrives. The pods of the Hungarian plant are small and ripen to a bright orange-red, a color which is retained through the drying and grinding process. Your box of imported Hungarian paprika will have the same brilliance as the ripe pepper pods. Its "sweet and noble" flavor will add charm to many a dish you never dreamed could be so glorified.

Paprika from Hungary is prized by discriminating cooks and gourmets of all nations. It is now grown extensively for export but in few countries is it used so profusely or with such tempting results as in its homeland. The Hungarian housewife does not sprinkle it on. She measures it by the teaspoon or tablespoon so that meats become a rich reddish-brown, soups have a rosy blush, and vegetables an added zest. Where we use paprika as a garnish, she uses it as an indispensable ingredient to give her dishes that piquant flavor and aroma so characteristic of good Hungarian food. Recently paprika has been elevated to scientific eminence as the bearer of vitamin C, but its spicy charm will probably always overshadow its nutritive value.

Sour cream is almost as characteristic of the Hungarian cuisine. Dishes which include it may also be made with the cultured variety now available in the United States. This looks like a whipped cream—is not really sour, only mildly tart—and adds a tang to meat, soup, vegetable, or dessert. Gentle heating neither thins nor curdles it. You will find that sour cream adds elegance to baked fish or meat, paprika chicken, a pancake entree, an egg or vegetable dish.

Hungarians love to dance to the music of the violin, cimbalom, clarinet, and viola. Their romantic music reflects the gaiety and the sadness of the people, the beauty and the pageantry of their village ceremonials, the swift spirit of hospitality and their pleasure in companionship. Coffeehouses have played a very special part in this friendly association. Excellent coffee, diluted with hot milk, is served for breakfast, but after dinner it is drunk black. For afternoon refreshment it is served with whipped cream.

Though the Magyars who settled the country a thousand years ago adopted much of the culture and religion of the West, they retained many of their own traditions—their distinctive costumes and festive celebrations. The splendor of the Hungarian peasantry in gala attire is exceeded only by their lavish feasts. Every holiday calls for its own feast. Typical are the saints' days, which in many parts of the country serve to commemorate events connected with the growing and harvesting of food.

On Shrove Tuesday vegetables are planted, poppy seed sown, and maize shelled for spring planting, a long day of work and merrymaking, with pancakes the traditional fare. At midnight, with the sounding of bells, the merriment ends; the gypsies silence their music and all return home. In Catholic communities, Ash Wednesday, the beginning of Lent, marks not only days of fasting but also the cessation of games and dancing and, in some villages, the exchange of the bright embroidered skirts of the womenfolk for somber dark ones. Even the little girls' vivid hair bows are replaced by soberer colors.

After Lent, Easter week holds much significance for these people. The first vegetables of the season are eaten on Green Thursday following Palm Sunday. Preparations for the Easter feast are completed on Good Friday with Easter cakes baked and Easter eggs painted. Cooking is ended and the fire allowed to go out. It will not be lighted again until after the chime of the bells on Holy Saturday, signifying the breaking of the fast. Then comes the bountiful Easter Eve supper. Throughout Hungary, Easter dinner is one of the most important feasts of the year. In fact the Hungarian word for Easter, *Húsvét*, means "taking of meat." The Easter menu includes a chicken soup, baked ham or pork, and roast lamb. There may be liver dumplings or noodles in the soup. Stuffed cabbage, also with meat, a green salad, cake, and black coffee will complete the meal.

St. Stephen's Day, August twentieth, the birthday of the first king of Hungary, is nationally observed with a special holiday meal and an entire week of celebration.

Shepherds are engaged or discharged on St. George's Day (April twenty-third). According to Alexander F. Károlyi in his *Hungarian Pageant*, flocks are rounded up then and this, too, calls for a feast. All Saints' Day, November first, is the last day of the sowing of the winter wheat. Both the end of the planting and the harvesting are significant events, usually followed by feasting and merriment. Then comes the Vintage Festival, a long and joyous affair which follows the gathering of the grapes in mid-October. A month later the grape juice has turned into new wine and is ready for the drinking at the St. Martin's fairs. Grapes grow in profusion on the hills and wine making is an important industry. From Hungary, fruit brandies and wines are now exported to all parts of the world. Wine is, of course, the national drink. One of the folk songs goes:

The Slovaks all drink brandy,
The Germans all drink beer,
The Hungarians drink wine only,
The very best, my dear.

The Christmas season is one of the most richly celebrated of all the Hungarian holidays. The day before Christmas is a fast day which ends on Christmas Eve with the exchange of gifts, singing around a decorated pine tree, and a special meal of paprika fish with potato purée, nut or poppy seed noodles, and fruit. As in America, the Christmas dinner features turkey if it can be afforded. In addition to the turkey, which has been fattened on walnuts and stuffed with chestnuts, there will be ragout soup of turkey, roast potatoes, stuffed cabbage, plums stuffed with almonds and preserved in red wine, orange salad, nut and poppy seed cakes.

In the more modest homes a typical Christmas Eve supper is likely to consist of cold ham, potato salad, and freshly baked cake. And for the feast dinner there will be chicken soup with noodles and, instead of turkey, roast chicken served with gooseberry sauce. For dessert, the traditional noodles and cakes, both made with nuts and poppy seeds.

Of all gala occasions, the celebration of a wedding is the most wonderful. There is always a fine banquet. If perchance a guest should praise the host's table, the host (the *groom's* father) would reply modestly: "We are poor but we live well!" Unbelievable quantities of poultry, a whole calf, a pig, a lamb, and perhaps a steer are made ready on the day before the wedding. On the festive day soups, meat dishes, pastries, and cakes are prepared in the big family kitchens or over open fireplaces. An enormous wedding cake with fancy decorations may be added to the feast in a wealthy household.

In some districts the wedding banquet starts with fruit plucked from the "Tree of Life," a bough hung with apples and nuts. This is followed by innumerable courses, one following the other in ceremonial succession from early afternoon until midnight. In other regions an interesting custom demands the presence in the banquet room at midnight of the women who have prepared the meal *and* their utensils. They perform the cooks' dance and a collection is taken for them. Dancing and feasting go on until dawn or—in wealthy households—until the supply of food and drink is exhausted. Wedding banquets of three days' duration are by no means unheard of!

The lavish tables of the feast days are in notable contrast to those of the daily routine. Even a holiday is often more simply observed in many homes. A middle-class Hungarian housewife can always please her family with goulash or paprikás veal or chicken accompanied frequently by sour cream. The vegetables may be stuffed peppers or stuffed cabbage and the dessert plum dumplings or *palacsinta* (pancakes) filled with jam, cottage cheese, or nuts. Suppers may be as simple as thick soup and poppy seed noodles or lentil soup with smoked pork or sausage. These foods, for which recipes are given in these pages, never fail to look attractive or be pleasing to the taste.

However, not all Hungarians eat so well for a

Poor man's fate is poverty;
Potato is his dinner
Squash is his supper. . . .

The field laborer, for instance, will have an early breakfast of bread and bacon with coffee or brandy. He will take with him to the field cheese, onion, and more bread by way of a second breakfast. At noon his wife carries him goulash soup with *much* bread. In the evening with his family he will partake of a meal of thick soup and corn-meal mush. Or perhaps there will be paprikás liver and blood sausage and cabbage with noodle squares. But however meager the meal, it will be prepared "with the heart" and will be both enjoyable and enjoyed.

Rich or poor, on every table will be the fragrant loaves of bread made with the rich, glutinous, unbleached flour that is Hungary's pride. *Metélt* (noodles), *galuska* (soft noodles), *csipetke* (pinched noodles), *tarhonya* (egg barley), and *gombóc* (dumplings) are basic foods made from this flour, as are strudels, pancakes, pastries, and other desserts. Fruits, raw or cooked, are used liberally by all classes and are made into jams and preserves for winter treats.

TYPICAL FEAST-DAY MENUS

For the special holiday feasts, Hungarians have their special and significant menus. Symbolism prompts the serving of special foods on certain days. Elek Magyar, in his *Hungarian Gourmet Master's Cookbook*, points out that New Year's Eve supper will include hare, venison, or "winged" poultry to "run or fly away with the old year's troubles." For dinner on New Year's Day, a roast suckling pig is presented to "boost with its snout the good luck of the New Year." Ash Wednesday calls for sour eggs and herring salad; Good Friday, a wine-flavored soup, stuffed eggs, and fish. "Blessed ham" makes its appearance on Easter Eve. On Easter Sunday baby lamb is roasted and there are sure to be many sorts of fancy cakes. Pentecost dinner will be of young goose with sour cream cucumbers and, for dessert, cherry strudel.

In olden days, during the forty days of Lent, fasting from Ash Wednesday until the Saturday before Easter was kept rigidly. Fatty foods and especially meat were prohibited. The custom was carried so far that all pots and pans in which greasy foods or meats had been cooked were stored away. Even dogs were compelled to fast, being deprived of their customary bones. But on Easter and until Friday of that week they had plenty of bones because of the vast amount of ham and lamb that had been consumed. Then, however, came meatless Friday again. So the legend grew that the dogs who had been feasting all the week until that day suddenly became scared, believing that forty boneless days were in store for them again. That is why many Hungarians call the first Friday after Easter, "Dog-scaring Friday."

Even the village folk will have their special menus for the holy days. Though their menus are less elaborate, they, too, take great pride and joy in their baking. Poppy seed cakes and nut cakes abound at Christmas; carnival doughnuts at New Year's; layer cakes for the Easter season. Except for the holy days, weddings, pig-killings, and grape harvests, village fare is likely to be plain and monotonous. The people live mostly on their own produce. A hearty soup may be the entire meal. Beef goulash or mutton stew is served repeatedly, or stuffed cabbage or peppers. Those villagers who raise chickens have seared chicken (with paprika) or, if there is sour cream, paprika chicken. They know how to make rich and varied desserts which they serve on special occasions but they are quite content with corn-meal mush or plum dumplings as everyday desserts.

Menus for Feast Days

CHRISTMAS EVE SUPPER

Sturgeon with Mashed Potatoes
Nut or Poppy Seed Noodles
Fresh Fruit

CHRISTMAS DINNER

Roast Turkey
Roast Potatoes
Savoy Cabbage, Chestnuts
Sliced Orange Salad
Poppy Seed and Nut Cakes

NEW YEAR'S EVE SUPPER

Bouillon
Roast Capon
Mashed Potatoes
Carrots
Cauliflower
Chestnut Cream

NEW YEAR'S DAY DINNER

Roast Suckling Pig, Garnishes
Roast Potatoes and Cucumbers
Carnival Doughnuts Filled with Raspberry Jam
Apples, Oranges, Nuts

LENTEN SEASON MEALS

Midday Dinner

Kohlrabi Soup
Egg Barley
Fruit Compote

•

Caraway Seed Soup
Spinach Pudding

Supper

Pale Tomato Soup
Pancakes, Cottage Cheese Filling

•

Sour Egg Soup, Egg Noodles

GOOD FRIDAY DINNER

Fish Soup or Apple Soup
Stuffed Eggs, Horseradish
Braised Fish
Curled Fritters

EASTER SUNDAY DINNER

Meat Soup, Liver Dumplings
Roast Ham and Potatoes, Pot Cheese
Creamed Sorrel and Radishes
Dobos Torte

•

EASTER SUNDAY DINNER

Roast Lamb, Mashed Potatoes
Green Peas
Stuffed Lettuce
Cream Puffs, Whipped Cream

EVERYDAY MEALS

While village families have for breakfast smoked or paprika bacon and bread, most city folk eat less. Their usual breakfast is coffee and a roll, perhaps with butter, jam, or honey. The more complete breakfast of ham and eggs, tea and toast is served in sophisticated homes and is referred to as the English breakfast.

A ten o'clock morning snack or tiffin is customary everywhere. Children take theirs to school and eat it at recess. Office workers and businessmen go to a nearby restaurant for a "small goulash."

As in other countries of Central Europe, Hungarian meals have their culmination in midday dinner. It is the heaviest meal of the day and the entire family comes home for it. Afternoon coffee or tea will include small cakes or cookies if there are guests, but only coffeecake when the family is alone. Many a graceful figure

is lost to these sweets. Whether at home or away, the Hungarian day is filled with opportunities for eating. Businessmen gather in the coffeehouses for a leisurely pickup. Sumptuous confectioneries are crowded with stylish shoppers. There is no fear of spoiling the appetite for supper, a much lighter meal, since it will not be served until eight or nine o'clock.

Everyday Menus

BREAKFAST

Coffee
Rolls or Bread
Butter, Jam, or Honey

•

Hard Boiled Eggs
Cold Ham
Rolls or Toast
Butter, Jam, or Honey
Tea with Lemon or Milk

TEN O'CLOCK SNACK

Buttered Bread
Salami and Rings of Green Pepper

•

Sardines on Buttered Roll

•

Small Goulash with Beer

MIDDAY MEAL AT HOME

Meat Soup with Noodles
Boiled Beef with Tomato Sauce
Parsley Potatoes
Cauliflower with Cream
Apple Strudel
Mineral Water

•

Bean Soup with Pinched Noodles
Pork Chops with Sauerkraut
Plum Dumplings

•

Beef Goulash with Potatoes
Cherry Strudel

AFTERNOON COFFEE FOR A GUEST

Coffee Half and Half, Whipped Cream
Chocolate Torte
Assorted Little Cakes and Biscuits

SUPPER

Roast Goose Liver
Mashed Potatoes
Eggplant Salad
Cabbage Noodles
Grapes, New Walnuts, Pears
Tea Mineral Water

•

Stuffed Cabbage
Pot Cheese Noodles
Fruit

•

Goulash Soup
Golden Dumplings

SUNDAY DINNER

Mushroom Soup
Layer Ham Pancakes
Breaded Chicken
Carrots
Green Beans
Parsley Potatoes
Cucumber Salad
Cherry Strudel
Mineral Water
Wine

SUNDAY SUPPER

Pale Tomato Soup
Skillet Steak
Stuffed Cabbage
Cheese Strudel
Fresh Fruit
Mineral Water
Wine
Cognac

APPETIZERS

APPETIZERS

The fragrant, tempting aroma that escapes from the preparation of a holiday meal in Hungary needs little else to tempt the appetite. Perhaps this is the reason that appetizers play a minor part in Hungarian meals. Those Hungarians who have traveled abroad have become familiar with the Scandinavian Smörgåsbord or the French hors d'oeuvres. Both have been adopted, or perhaps adapted, by city restaurants and hotels in Hungary, but in private homes native taste treats are served.

All kinds of pâté—meat, liver, game, fowl—are served and, of course, caviar from the *kecsege* (sturgeon). This fresh-water fish produces unsurpassed caviar, which, though rinsed in salt water to clean and preserve it, does not become salty and retains, undisguised, its fresh flavor, the gourmet's delight. A fish salad often opens the meal, as do steamed or roast goose liver, served cold, or stuffed goose neck (or turkey). Chilled baked green peppers in vinegar, eggs with horseradish, fried cheese, or ham biscuits make memorable appetizers but even those cannot compare with ham-, chicken-, or lobster-filled pancakes. (Recipes for all these delicacies follow, or are given in Chapters on "Pancakes" and "Strudels and Pastries.")

Spring adds fresh radishes and green onions to the list, and in season cantaloupe is served. Károly Gundel, in his Hungarian book, *The Art of Hospitality*, tells how to eat it for increased enjoyment. He says the fork should be pierced into a whole lemon before each bite of melon. Then the oil of the lemon rind, as well as the tart juice, will enhance the cantaloupe flavor. When there is melon, no other appetizer is offered.

CHILLED BAKED GREEN PEPPERS IN VINEGAR

SÜLT PAPRIKA

6 SERVINGS

6 sweet green peppers
3 tablespoons vinegar
¼ teaspoon salt
⅛ teaspoon pepper
1 tablespoon oil (optional)

Wash, clean, and dry the green peppers. Heat in a moderate oven (350° F.) for 10 minutes. Blend the vinegar, salt, pepper, and oil. Remove the peppers from the oven and peel off and discard the thin skins. Cool and slice into ¼-inch rings. Serve with the mixed dressing.

STEAMED OR ROAST* GOOSE LIVER

SÜLT LIBAMÁJ

6 SERVINGS

2 tablespoons goose fat
1 large goose liver
¼ teaspoon salt
⅛ teaspoon pepper or paprika

Place goose liver in fat. Sprinkle with salt and pepper or paprika

*Roast (*sült* in Hungarian) does not necessarily mean oven-cooked.

and add 2 tablespoons water. Then cover and let steam for half an hour. Remove cover and increase the heat to brown the liver. Do not overcook; it should remain tender. Serve hot with rice or cold, sliced, as an appetizer.

STUFFED GOOSE NECK

TÖLTÖTT LIBANYAK

5 SERVINGS

½ cup ground goose meat
½ cup ground veal
½ cup ground beef
1 clove garlic, finely chopped
1 moistened baker's roll
2 onions, finely chopped
1 whole uncooked skin from goose neck
Meat broth or water
3 tablespoons butter or other fat
1 tablespoon flour
1 tablespoon lemon juice
Salt and pepper
2 eggs
1 bay leaf
6 peppercorns
1 carrot, sliced

Mix together ground goose meat, veal, and beef. Add garlic, moistened roll, and chopped onion. Melt the butter or fat and add flour. Stir until golden brown, then thin with 2 tablespoons broth or water, stirring until smooth. Now add the meat mixture, lemon juice, and salt and pepper to taste, blending all together. Let simmer until moisture is absorbed and meat is tender. Cool. Add eggs. Fill goose neck loosely and sew up the ends. Brown until crisp in fat or butter; or cook for 30 minutes in water, to which a bay leaf, peppercorns, and sliced carrot have been added. Serve hot, sliced diagonally in ½-inch pieces.

Note: Turkey neck is equally good prepared in this manner.

LIPTÓI CHEESE SPREAD

KŐRÖZÖTT LIPTÓI

1 CUP

½ pound liptói or cream cheese
¼ pound butter
½ teaspoon sweet paprika
½ teaspoon prepared mustard
½ teaspoon caraway seeds
1 teaspoon chopped chives
1 teaspoon chopped capers
Dark bread

Blend cheese and butter. Mix in the seasonings. Spread on thinly sliced dark bread or on crackers.

GOOSE LIVER BAKED IN MILK

TEJBENSÜLT LIBAMÁJ

6 SERVINGS

1 piece of goose or other fat
1 goose liver
½ cup milk
¼ teaspoon salt
½ teaspoon paprika

Put a piece of goose fat in bottom of a deep pan. Place goose liver on top of the goose fat. Cover with slightly salted fresh milk and let stand overnight. Cook, covered, until milk is absorbed. Remove lid, then brown liver gently on both sides, and watch to avoid scorching. Serve hot with mashed potatoes or cold, sliced, and sprinkled with paprika, as an appetizer.

FRIED CHEESE

KIRÁNTOTT SAJT

This is excellent as an entree following the soup course, or with a salad for supper.

6 SERVINGS

6 slices (¼ inch thick) mild hard cheese
2 eggs, slightly beaten
1 cup fine bread crumbs
2 tablespoons bacon fat

Dip the cheese slices into the egg. Coat with crumbs and brown lightly in the hot fat. Turn to brown both sides. Serve immediately.

MEAT PÂTÉ OR PASTE WITH TARTARE SAUCE

HÚSPÁSTÉTOM TATÁRMÁRTÁSSAL

4 CUPS

2-pound chicken, cooked and boned
1½ pounds veal, roasted
1 can sardines in oil
½ cup cooked ham
2 hard-boiled eggs, finely chopped
Juice of 1 lemon
1 teaspoon prepared mustard
½ teaspoon salt

Grind the chicken, veal, sardines, and ham. Stir and grind again.

Combine well with eggs, lemon juice, mustard, and salt. Use as a spread for delicate sandwiches or serve with brown rolls.

EGGS WITH HORSERADISH

TOJÁS TORMÁVAL

6 SERVINGS

6 hard-cooked eggs, sliced
¼ cup french dressing
1 tablespoon grated horseradish
Paprika

Arrange the sliced eggs on a platter. Sprinkle with the french dressing and dot with the horseradish. Garnish with paprika.

HAM BISCUITS

SONKÁSFÁNK

This is a tempting appetizer, or it may be served as a main dish.

12 SMALL OR
6 LARGE SERVINGS

2 tablespoons butter
2 tablespoons fine bread crumbs
½ cup sour cream
2 tablespoons grated cheese
¾ cup finely chopped boiled ham
3 eggs, separated
Sour cream for garnish

Mix together the butter and crumbs; add sour cream, cheese, ham, and egg yolks, and blend well. Beat egg whites stiff and fold ham mixture into them. Pour onto a greased baking sheet. Do not spread. Bake in a moderate oven (350° F.) until set and golden brown, about 20 minutes. Spread with additional sour cream if desired and return to oven for 5 minutes. Cut in small squares or with biscuit cutter: serve hot.

SOUPS

SOUPS

Soups play an important role in the eating habits of the Hungarian family. Many a hostess, cook, or "consumer" would put a good soup at the top of the list of favorite dishes. Hearty soups are basic in the workingman's meals and frequently there is little else. The variety is as limitless as the cook's imagination is capable of dreaming up, for there are many ingredients available for making soup either a hearty, invigorating food or a well-blended extract of delicate flavor and aroma.

Cold fruit soups are favorites. Clear, thin, fragrant soups such as bouillon, consommé, and the festive Hungarian queen's or chicken soup start the meal at the tables of the well to do and are considered essential for special occasions. An important Hungarian soup is the *gulyásleves* or goulash soup—actually a goulash with a "long" (thin) gravy—rich with meat, slowly cooked, and seasoned with onions and paprika. Often served as a whole meal, a large plate of this meaty soup eaten hot with *csipetke* (pinched noodles), *tarhonya* (egg barley), or potatoes is heartening and sustaining.

The making of a good soup requires care, unhurried cooking

which will draw out the flavor from the meat and bones, and skill in the blending of subtle seasonings. Agnes Zilahy says in her *Hungarian Cookbook* (1891): "Many a soup could be vastly improved by browning finely chopped mixed vegetables in fat or butter, or by adding—discreetly—onion, garlic or paprika."

Seasonings other than paprika which give an unusual zest to Hungarian soups are dill, bay leaf, caraway seeds, and whole peppercorns. Lemon juice or vinegar is sometimes used for a mild pungent taste, and cream will give the dish mellowness. Sour cream, always a favorite, is added when a somewhat tart flavor is desired. Usually soups made with browned thickening get a spoonful of sour cream in the serving bowl. Instead of cream, sliced hard-cooked eggs, chopped green peppers or parsley, frankfurter slices, or croutons may be used as decoration.

Soft noodles, pinched noodles, and dumplings in many forms are also added to soups or are cooked in the broths. Dumpling varieties include ham or liver, marrow or meat balls, farina balls, and a soft noodle dough cut off into the hot liquid—the last making tiny dumplings when cooked.

In Hungary, bread, never crackers, is served with soup, and there is rarely butter.

COLD RASPBERRY SOUP

HIDEG MÁLNALEVES
6 SERVINGS

1 pound raspberries
½ cup granulated sugar

Wash, clean, and crush fresh raspberries. Cover with sugar and let stand for several hours. Press through strainer. Chill. Stir before serving. Sprinkle Rice Krispies or popcorn over each serving, to add contrast to soup.

COLD APPLE SOUP

HIDEG ALMALEVES

6 SERVINGS

4 apples, pared and diced
½ cup sugar
Rind of 1 lemon, finely chopped
3 cups hot water
½ cup red or white wine
2 tablespoons flour
2 tablespoons cold water
½ cup heavy cream

Combine the apples, sugar, lemon rind, and hot water. Cook until apples are tender. Add the wine. Blend the flour and cold water until smooth. Thin with a few tablespoons of the hot soup. Then mix into the soup. Simmer 5 minutes. Chill, and add cream before serving.

COLD TOMATO SOUP WITH WINE

HIDEG PARADICSOMLEVES BORRAL

6 SERVINGS

3 cups tomato juice
2 cups white wine
3 tablespoons sugar
2 hard-cooked eggs, sliced

Combine the tomato juice, wine, and sugar. Heat to blend. Chill. Serve with floating slices of egg.

Note: In season, use fresh uncooked tomatoes pressed through a strainer to make 3 cups of pulp and juice. Replace the eggs with ½ cup of heavy cream, whipped. Float a spoonful in each bowl of soup.

COLD SOUR-SWEET CHERRY SOUP

HIDEG MEGGY-ÉS CSERESZNYELEVES

6 SERVINGS

2 pounds sour cherries, pitted
1 cup or more sugar
1 stick cinnamon
3 cups water
2 tablespoons flour
1 cup heavy cream
1 cup red wine

Simmer the cherries, sugar, and cinnamon in the water until the cherries are tender. Remove the cinnamon. Blend the flour with 3 tablespoons of cold water until smooth. Thin with 3 more tablespoons of water and stir into the hot soup. Heat to boiling. Chill. Before serving, stir in the cream and the wine.

BEAN SOUP WITH PINCHED NOODLES

BABLEVES CSIPETKÉVEL

8 SERVINGS

2 cups dry beans
6 cups water
2 carrots, chopped
1 tablespoon chopped parsley
1 teaspoon salt
Pinched Noodles
1 cup sour cream

Soak the beans overnight. Drain, rinse with cold water, and drain again. Add the water, carrots, parsley, and salt. Cook slowly for 2 hours, or until tender. Strain if desired. Pinch off bits of noodle dough, the size of a hazelnut, into the boiling soup. Cook until tender. Stir in the sour cream and serve.

CARAWAY SEED SOUP

KÖMÉNYMAGOS LEVES

1 tablespoon caraway seeds
½ teaspoon salt
6 cups boiling water
3 tablespoons bacon fat
4 tablespoons flour
½ cup sour cream
½ cup croutons

6 SERVINGS

Combine the caraway seeds, salt, and water. Simmer for 15 minutes. Blend the fat and flour. Add 2 cups of the soup, and stir until thick and smooth. Combine with the remaining soup and heat to boiling. Divide the cream equally in the soup bowls. Pour the soup over it. Serve with croutons floating on top.

LENTIL SOUP

LENCSELEVES

1 pound lentils
6 cups water
1 cup smoked pork or ham
1 teaspoon salt
1 carrot
1 sprig parsley
1 onion, finely chopped
1 knob celery, sliced
2 tablespoons flour
2 tablespoons bacon fat
¼ cup sour cream

6 SERVINGS

Soak the lentils several hours or overnight. Drain and add the water. Add the meat, salt, carrot, parsley, onion, and celery. Cook slowly until the lentils and vegetables are soft. Remove the meat. Strain the soup, rubbing the lentils and vegetables through the strainer. Brown the flour in the fat; stir in a cup of the soup, and cook until thick and smooth. Add the rest of the soup and more water, if needed for a pleasing consistency. Add cream, heat and serve in wide soup bowls.

SPLIT PEA SOUP

SZÁRITOTT BORSÓLEVES

Follow the preceding recipe but use split peas instead of lentils. Or use fresh peas, and do not soak.

CABBAGE SOUP

KÁPOSZTALEVES

6 SERVINGS

2 cups shredded green cabbage
1½ teaspoons salt
⅛ teaspoon pepper or
1 teaspoon paprika
¼ cup bacon fat
4 cups water
3 cups diced potatoes
1 ripe tomato, skinned and chopped

Combine the cabbage, salt, and pepper or paprika. Brown in the bacon fat. Add the water and potatoes, and cook for 15 minutes, or until the vegetables are nearly tender. Add the tomato and cook 5 minutes longer.

KOHLRABI SOUP

KALARÁBÉLEVES

1 small cut-up chicken
4 young kohlrabi
1¼ teaspoons salt

2 tablespoons chopped parsley
4 tablespoons butter or lard
3 tablespoons flour
2 egg yolks
½ cup cream

8 TO 12 SERVINGS

Cook the chicken for 30 minutes in salted water to cover. Peel the kohlrabi and cut into fine strips. Add to the chicken with the salt and continue cooking until chicken and kohlrabi are tender. Wilt the parsley in the fat; add the flour and blend. Stir in a cup of the soup and continue stirring and cooking until thick and smooth. Thin with the remaining soup.

Remove the chicken from bones and cut into bite-size pieces. Return to the soup, and heat to boiling. Mix the egg yolks with the cream, and stir into the hot soup. Serve at once.

MUSHROOM SOUP

GOMBALEVES

1 pound mushrooms, chopped
1 clove garlic
2 tablespoons chopped parsley
1 small onion, chopped
3 tablespoons butter
1 teaspoon salt
1 teaspoon paprika
3 tablespoons flour
4 cups chicken stock or water
½ cup sour cream or heavy sweet cream

6 SERVINGS

Brown the mushrooms, garlic, parsley, and onion in the butter. Stir in the salt, paprika, and flour. Add half the liquid. Stir until thick and smooth. Blend in the remaining liquid and heat to boiling. Divide the cream equally in the soup bowls, and pour the soup over it.

POTATO SOUP

BURGONYALEVES

4 medium-size potatoes, pared and cubed
2 carrots, diced
2 stalks celery, chopped
Boiling water
1 onion, finely chopped
1 tablespoon butter
2 egg yolks
1 cup sour cream
3 frankfurters, cut in small pieces
1 cup toast cubes

6 SERVINGS

Combine the potatoes, carrots, and celery. Cover with boiling water and cook until tender. Brown the onion in the butter, and add to the vegetables. Remove from the stove. Press all through a strainer. Reheat. Mix the egg yolks and cream. Add the frankfurter pieces. Pour the hot soup over the cream mixture. Without stirring, ladle into warm soup bowls. Garnish with toast cubes.

SAUERKRAUT SOUP

KORHELYLEVES

2 cups sauerkraut, finely chopped
4 cups water
1 small onion, finely chopped
3 tablespoons bacon fat
½ teaspoon paprika
½ pound sausage meat

3 tablespoons flour
6 SERVINGS *½ cup sour cream*

Boil the sauerkraut in the water until tender. Brown the onion in the fat; add the paprika. Shape the sausage into tiny balls and brown in the fat with the onions and paprika. Remove from the fat to the boiling soup. Stir the flour into the fat remaining in the pan. Thin with a cup of the soup, and stir until thickened. Add another cup of the soup and blend. Combine with the sauerkraut. Heat to boiling and serve topped with a tablespoon of cream on each bowl.

PALE TOMATO SOUP

FEHÉR PARADICSOMLEVES

5 cups clear chicken broth
½ teaspoon salt
8 ripe tomatoes
Croutons

6 SERVINGS

Combine the broth, salt, and whole tomatoes. Simmer gently for an hour. Remove the tomatoes and strain. The soup should remain clear. Serve with croutons.

TOMATO SOUP WITH HAM

PARADICSOMLEVES SONKÁVAL

1 ham bone with some meat
3 carrots, cut in strips
3 onions, sliced
1 white turnip, sliced
10 medium-size ripe tomatoes
½ teaspoon salt
10 peppercorns
Croutons

6 SERVINGS

Cook together the ham bone, carrots, onions, and turnip with water to cover for about an hour. Add the tomatoes, salt, and peppercorns and simmer for half and hour. Strain and serve with croutons.

SPINACH SOUP

SPENÓTLEVES

1 pound well-washed spinach
4 cups water
½ teaspoon salt
2 small onions, finely chopped
2 tablespoons fat
3 tablespoons flour
1 cup cream
2 hard-cooked eggs, sliced

6 SERVINGS

Simmer the spinach until soft in the salted water. Strain (save the water), and rub the spinach to a pulp through the strainer. Brown the onions in the fat, add the flour, and blend. Stir in a cup of the spinach liquid and cook, stirring, until thick and smooth. Add the remaining liquid and the spinach. Heat to boiling. Remove from the fire and blend in the cream. Serve in soup bowls and garnish with the egg slices.

QUEEN'S SOUP OR CHICKEN SOUP

KIRALYNÉ LEVES

This soup is served as a separate course at special-occasion dinners. It is considered one of the finest soups made.

1 stewing chicken, cut up
½ pound soup beef

1 calf's foot
2 teaspoons salt
⅓ cup rice
Croutons

10 SERVINGS

Simmer the chicken, beef, and calf's foot, in water to cover, for about 3 hours. Add the salt and cook another hour, or until meat is tender. Remove the chicken, beef, and all bones. Add the rice slowly to the boiling soup, and cook until very soft.

Meanwhile, remove the chicken and beef from bones and grind it. Drain rice and save the liquid. Mix the rice with the meat, and grind again. Combine with the soup. Strain all through a coarse sieve, rubbing the meat and rice through also. Reheat and serve with croutons.

Variation: Omit the beef, calf's foot, and rice. Grind and add only the white meat of the chicken. Add 2 hard-cooked eggs and 2 sliced and toasted baker's rolls. Press through a strainer and reheat.

FISH SOUP

HALLEVES

2 potatoes, pared and diced
2 carrots, diced
1 knob celery, diced
1½ teaspoons salt
8 cups boiling water
1 large baker's roll, soaked in milk
2 pounds codfish fillets
1 tablespoon chopped parsley
2 eggs

6 to 8 SERVINGS

Cook the potatoes, carrots, and celery with 1 teaspoon of the salt in the boiling water, until nearly tender. Reserve the liquid. Grind the raw fish with the cooked vegetables. Add the parsley, ½ teaspoon of salt, the eggs, and the roll. Mix and press with a spoon into small dumplings. Carefully drop into the boiling soup, cover, and cook slowly until fish is done, about 15 minutes.

BEEF SOUP

MARHAHÚS LEVES

4 pounds beef shank or rump
1½ pounds beef bones
2 teaspoons salt
15 peppercorns
1 onion, sliced
3 carrots, sliced
1 tomato, sliced
1 knob celery, sliced
½ kohlrabi
1 sprig parsley with root
½ pound Fine Noodles, cooked

8 SERVINGS

Cook beef and bones in a large kettle, covered with water, for 1 hour. Add the salt, peppercorns, and vegetables, and cook slowly for 3½ hours, or until the vegetables are soft and the meat falls from the bones. Cool and remove the fat. Strain the soup, add the noodles reheat, and serve.

PIG NECK SOUP

ORJALEVES

This soup is prepared. in Hungary, at the Feast of the Celebration of Pig-Killing.

Use pig's neck instead of the beef in the Beef Soup, above. Omit the noodles, and serve with Liver Dumplings, given below.

8 SERVINGS

LIVER DUMPLINGS

MÁJGOMBÓC

12 TO 15 DUMPLINGS

1 small onion, chopped
1 tablespoon butter
1 large baker's roll, moistened with milk
¼ pound fowl, calf, beef, or pork liver, ground
1 tablespoon chopped parsley
½ teaspoon salt
⅛ teaspoon pepper
2 eggs
½ cup bread crumbs
Soup stock

Wilt the onion in the butter in a heavy frying pan. Press excess milk from the roll, crumble, and combine with the onions. Add the liver, parsley, salt, pepper, eggs, and bread crumbs. Blend well. With floured hands, shape into walnut-size dumplings and drop into the soup stock, brought to a boil. Cook 10 minutes.

Note: Marrow Balls and Ham Dumplings are made in this same manner. Use ½ cup of bone marrow instead of the liver, when making Marrow Balls. For the Ham Dumplings, use 1 cup of cooked ham instead of the liver.

UJHÁZY SOUP

UJHÁZY LEVES

1 large stewing chicken, cut up
1 pound rump beef
1 pound beef bones
5–6 cockscombs
Soup greens
¼ head savoy cabbage
1 green pepper
5 mushrooms
1 ripe tomato
4 or 5 flowerets cauliflower
½ cup peas
½ cup cut-up string beans
Chives
½ pound Fine Noodles, cooked

12 OR MORE SERVINGS

Cook chicken, meat and bones, covered with water, in large kettle for half an hour. Add cut-up soup greens, cut-up savoy cabbage, green pepper cut in rings, and the remaining vegetables. Salt and pepper to taste. Simmer for 3 hours. When meat falls from bones, strain mixture. Cut chicken in small pieces. Put back into strained soup, together with some of the strained vegetables, and the cooked noodles. Heat and serve garnished with chives.

Serve beef, sliced, with horseradish as a separate dish.

FARINA BALLS

DARAGALUSKA

2 tablespoons butter
2 eggs
4 tablespoons farina
½ teaspoon salt

6 SERVINGS

In a bowl cream butter, add eggs, and stir until creamy. Add farina and salt, stirring constantly until mixture is smooth. With a teaspoon make small dumplings like soft noodles and drop into boiling soup. Cook for 15 minutes, or until done.

GOULASH SOUP

GULYÁSLEVES

2 medium-size onions, chopped
2 tablespoons fat
2 pounds beef, cut in small pieces
1 small heart, cubed
½ pound liver, cubed
2 teaspoons salt
1 tablespoon paprika
2 green peppers, sliced
2 tomatoes, sliced
1 carrot, diced
1 sprig parsley, chopped
2 potatoes, pared and diced
Pinched Noodles

8 TO 10 SERVINGS

Brown the onion in the fat. Add the beef, heart, and liver, and stir until well browned. Add the salt, paprika, peppers, tomatoes, carrot, and parsley. Pour on water to cover and cook slowly until the meat is tender, about 2½ hours. Add the potatoes and cook 20 minutes, or until potatoes are tender. Serve with the noodles, freshly cooked in boiling salted water.

MOCK GOULASH SOUP

HAMIS GULYÁSLEVES

"Poor man's goulash soup" is made without the meat, indicated in the preceding recipe. The vegetables are cooked in leftover meat stock, with water added as needed. It, too, is served with Pinched Noodles.

RAGOUT SOUP

RAGÚLEVES

2 chicken gizzards
2 chicken livers
2 chicken hearts
1 cup sweetbreads
2 stalks celery
2 carrots
1½ teaspoons salt
5 peppercorns
5 cups water
½ cup chopped mushrooms
2 tablespoons butter
3 tablespoons flour
2 egg yolks
1 cup sweet cream

6 SERVINGS

Combine the chicken giblets, sweetbreads, celery, carrots, salt, peppercorns, and water. Cook slowly, replacing water as needed, until all ingredients are tender. Remove and discard the celery and carrots. Chop the giblets and sweetbreads, and return to the soup. Brown the mushrooms in the butter. Blend in the flour. Add a cup of the soup. Continue cooking and stirring until thickened and smooth. Thin with another cup of soup; then add to the soup mixture. Heat to boiling. Mix the egg yolks and cream. Divide equally into soup bowls; then pour on the hot soup.

SOUR EGG SOUP

SAVANYÚTOJÁS LEVES

6 SERVINGS

1 onion, finely chopped
2 tablespoons butter
2 tablespoons flour
1 teaspoon salt
3 cups boiling water
1 bay leaf
1 tablespoon lemon juice or vinegar
½ cup sour cream
6 poached eggs
Paprika

Brown the onion in the butter; blend in the flour and salt. Add 1 cup of the water and stir until thick and smooth. Add the rest of the water, the bay leaf, and lemon juice or vinegar. Simmer until nearly boiling. Blend in the sour cream. Serve in soup plates over individually poached eggs. Garnish with paprika.

"TAILOR'S COLLAR" SOUP

SZABÓGALLÉR LEVES

This is an economy dish served in village homes during Lent.

6 SERVINGS

1 onion, finely chopped
3 tablespoons olive oil
1 teaspoon paprika
2 teaspoons salt
¼ cup farina
1 cup flour
2 eggs
1 tablespoon water
6 cups boiling, salted water

Lightly brown the onion in the olive oil. Add the paprika, half the salt, and the farina. Stir until browned. Mix the flour, eggs, 1 tablespoon water, and the remaining salt into a stiff dough. Knead lightly and roll as thin as a knife blade. Place small spoonfuls of the farina mixture about 3 inches apart on the thin dough. Cut with a pastry cutter into 3-inch squares and fold each square into a triangle. Make sure the edges are sealed. Drop into the boiling, salted water and cook until tender, about 20 minutes.

MEATS

The Magyar nomads brought with them from the slopes of the Urals hardy livestock with the wild characteristics of their origin. The fierce-looking, long-horned cattle, gray-black sheep, and rugged hogs were the Magyar's primary food as well as his "stock in trade." The oxen became his servant, pulling his plow and his cart.

The significant place that animals held in Hungarian tradition is indicated by the celebrations that centered around them. One region long marked the New Year's arrival by the ceremony of "turning the herd around" so that it would survive and thrive. The strongest, fittest son in the family was chosen for this honored duty. Throughout the country the shepherds were hired on St. George's Day and a feast was held to send them off to their flocks in health and good cheer.

To this day, cattle, sheep, and pig raising have continued to be basic industries in Hungary. Meat is one of the most important of all native foods and the Hungarian cooks are perhaps best known for their meat dishes.

The national dish is *gulyás* or *gulyáshús*, which means herdsman's meat. It probably had its origin in the camps of the herdsmen, who cooked their meat and vegetables all together in black kettles over their campfires. Beef, green peppers, onions, potatoes, paprika, and salt are the usual ingredients.

Gulyás in one form or another is eaten in all countries but nowhere is it better than it is in Hungary. The secret is in the proportions of meat and paprika and in the gentle cooking, which preserves the aroma and flavor of the bright red, sharp or sweet spice that blends into the flavor and fragrance of the meat-vegetable combination. But searching for the *valódi* (genuine) *gulyás* recipe is as futile as attempting to resolve the riddle of what is the true American shortcake base—biscuit or cake. For instance, one group of *gulyás* gourmets sautés the paprika with the onions in the early preparation and adds tomatoes to the cooking meat; another scorns tomatoes and adds the paprika after all browning is done, insisting that frying temperatures destroy the aroma of the spice. Some finish the dish off with diced potatoes while others serve it minus potatoes but with *galuska* (soft noodles) or *csipetke* (pinched noodles). Whatever the method or additions, one thing is essential—good-quality, not too fat beef should be used in every *gulyás* recipe.

Though beef is the preferred meat in Hungary, pork is a close second, while bacon is an all-important staple of the peasant. It is of superior quality, coming as it does from carefully and properly fattened hogs. And as choice, when it comes to quality, is the whole roast pig which is prepared for a *tor* or feast. Fresh pork, like fresh beef, can be had in city shops the year round.

Village folk prepare their own meat for winter. Slaughtering day is a great day in the rural household, with family, neighbors, and relatives all participating. Through the long day they complete the butchering, prepare the liver and blood sausage, headcheese and pigs' feet, trim the hams and bacon sides for smoking, and render the lard. The day ends with the *tor*, a sumptuous meal shared and enjoyed by all the participants in the day's activities. It will start with *orjaleves* (pig neck soup) and liver dumplings or noodles. Cabbage will be stuffed with meat, sausages baked, and a rack of pork chops roasted. There will be *turóscsusza* (cottage cheese noodles) with fresh cracklings and of course the many cakes and pastries. Guests are frequently invited and the eating and drinking will go on until dawn.

Veal is a great delicacy in Hungary and comes from specially bred milk-fed calves. Breaded chops, veal fricassee, veal *pörkölt* (braised), or paprika veal, are the most popular veal dishes. *Pörkölt,* an all-meat dish cooked slowly with much paprika, takes no sour cream. The same dish *with* sour cream is called *paprikás.* It may also be made with chicken, mutton, or pork as substitutes.

Suckling lamb is used for roasts and the chops are widely used but mutton is not popular in city markets or on the tables of the well to do. Village folk, however, make excellent *pörkölt, paprikás,* and *tokány* (stew) from lamb and mutton. In the sheep-herding hills almost no other fresh meat is eaten. The shepherd is a traditional figure, and his food patterns are centuries old.

The Hungarian's skill with meat is based on his use of *good* meat and the slowness with which he cooks it. This is the secret of all successful meat cookery. The meat is richly seasoned, mellowed with cream or gravy, and served simply. The appetite takes care of the rest.

BEEF STEAK WITH MUSHROOMS

GOMBÁS ROSTÉLYOS

3 pounds round or rump steak
1 teaspoon salt
1/8 teaspoon pepper
1/4 cup bacon fat
2 strips bacon, chopped

2 onions, finely chopped
1 tablespoon chopped parsley
1 pound mushrooms, sliced
1 cup cooked tomatoes

8 SERVINGS

Sprinkle the beef with salt and pepper and pound it well. Brown quickly on both sides in bacon fat. Meanwhile fry the bacon strips; add onions, parsley, and mushrooms, and lightly brown. Combine the meat and mushroom mixture; add the tomatoes and simmer until the sauce is thick and the meat tender.

ESZTERHÁZY STEAK

ESZTERHÁZY ROSTÉLYOS

3 pounds round steak, cut 1-inch thick
1 teaspoon salt
1/8 teaspoon pepper
2 tablespoons fat
2 fresh tomatoes, sliced, or 1 cup canned tomatoes
1 cup sour cream

8 SERVINGS

Make cuts on steak edges about 2 inches apart, so meat will not curl. Sprinkle with salt and pepper, and brown on both sides in the fat. Add the tomatoes and simmer until the steak is tender. Add the sour cream; cover, cook for 5 minutes more, and serve.

GARLIC STEAK

FOKHAGYMÁS ROSTÉLYOS

3 pounds beefsteak, thinly sliced
1/2 teaspoon salt
1/8 teaspoon pepper
3 tablespoons olive oil

3 tablespoons fat
1 clove garlic, chopped
2 tablespoons chopped parsley

8 SERVINGS

Sprinkle the meat with salt and pepper. Cut into 8 serving pieces; place ½ tablespoon olive oil on each, stack, and let stand in refrigerator for 3 hours. Heat the fat, and quickly brown the meat in it, on both sides. Remove to platter. Add the garlic and parsley to the meat juices, stir, and pour over the meat.

SKILLET STEAK

SERPENYŐS ROSTÉLYOS

8 SERVINGS

2 tablespoons fat
3 pounds round steak, cut into servings
2 onions, sliced
1 tablespoon paprika

Heat the fat, brown the meat and onions in it, stir in the paprika. Cover and steam for 1 hour, turning when necessary to prevent overbrowning. A tablespoon of water may be added if steak becomes dry before it is tender.

ROAST BEEF DUMPLINGS

MARHAPECSENYE GOMBÓC

1½ cups steamed rice
2 pounds ground raw or cooked beef
1 teaspoon salt
⅛ teaspoon pepper
2 eggs
Grated rind of ½ lemon
4 strips bacon, chopped
¼ cup bacon fat

Juice of ½ lemon
½ cup sour cream

6 SERVINGS

Combine the rice, beef, salt, pepper, eggs, and lemon rind. Fry the bacon until crisp; then add and mix well. Form dumplings the size of an egg. Flatten these a little with a spoon. Then brown on both sides in hot bacon fat. Remove to a warm platter. Stir the lemon juice and sour cream into the fat to make a gravy.

GOULASH

GULYÁS

This is a favorite dish with Mrs. Willy Pogany, noted Hungarian hostess. She sets the stage for a dinner with a peasant atmosphere by serving it piping hot from an earthen casserole. With it she serves soft noodles or pinched noodles. With dill pickles, a green salad, dark bread, and good coffee, the meal is complete with or without dessert.

4 pounds beef (chuck or rump), cut in 2-inch pieces
2 strips bacon or salt pork or 2 tablespoons bacon fat
6 onions, coarsely chopped
3 tablespoons paprika
1½ teaspoons salt
2 green peppers, coarsely chopped

8 TO 10 SERVINGS

Brown half the beef in its own fat in a large skillet; transfer to a kettle or dutch oven and repeat with other half. Rinse the skillet with a cup of water and add the liquid to the meat. Cover and cook slowly over low heat.

Chop the bacon and fry in skillet; add the onions and brown

lightly. Stir in the paprika and salt; then combine with the simmering meat. Stir in the uncooked green peppers and continue cooking slowly for about 2 hours or until the meat is tender—*not* soft.

BREADED LAMB STEAKS

RÁNTOTT BÁRÁNY

8 half-pound lamb steaks or 8 shoulder chops
1 clove garlic
1 teaspoon salt
¼ teaspoon pepper
Flour
2 eggs, slightly beaten
Bread crumbs
½ cup fat

8 SERVINGS

Trim excess fat from the steaks or chops. Crush garlic and rub over meat; season pieces with salt and pepper and roll in flour. Dip in eggs, then in bread crumbs. Brown quickly on both sides in the hot fat. Turn heat low and continue cooking slowly, covered, until meat is tender, about 20 minutes.

CHEESE-BROILED LAMB CHOPS

ROSTONSÜLT BÁRÁNYKARAJ

This is a tempting dish. It should be served as soon as done, accompanied by steamed rice, a good green vegetable, and a tossed salad.

¾ cup grated cheese
½ cup fine bread crumbs

½ teaspoon salt
6 thin shoulder lamb chops
1 whole egg or
6 SERVINGS *2 egg yolks, beaten*

Mix together the cheese, bread crumbs, and salt. Using a pastry brush or spoon, coat the chops on both sides with egg, and dip in the cheese mixture. Arrange on a baking sheet and broil slowly, turning once. When cheese is melted and crumbs brown, the meat should be tender.

BREADED PIGS' KNUCKLES

KIRÁNTOTT SERTÉSCSÜLÖK

4 pounds pigs' knuckles
2 teaspoons salt
1 egg, slightly beaten
1 cup bread crumbs
½ cup fat

6 SERVINGS

Clean the knuckles and cook 10 minutes in enough boiling water to cover. Plunge into cold water and remove skins. Add the salt to the hot water and return the meat to it. Simmer until meat comes off the bones. Roll chunks of the meat in the egg, then in the crumbs, and brown quickly on each side in the hot fat.

PORK CHOPS WITH SAUERKRAUT

SERTÉSBORDA KÁPOSZTÁVAL

1 onion, finely chopped
2 tablespoons fat
1 teaspoon paprika
1 pound (2 cups) sauerkraut
½ teaspoon salt

6 thin pork chops
1 cup sour cream
6 SERVINGS *¼ cup chopped dill pickle*

Cook the onion in the fat until golden. Add the paprika and sauerkraut; cover and simmer while the chops are browning. Salt the chops and flatten with a mallet. Brown slowly on each side in their own fat. Place on top of the sauerkraut and cook together for 1 hour. Five minutes before serving, stir the sour cream into the sauerkraut. Serve the chops on top of it, and garnish each one with the dill pickle.

ROAST SUCKLING PIG

SÜLT MALAC

In Hungary, roast suckling pig is traditional for New Year's dinner. It will have a red apple in its mouth, and be served with red cabbage and egg barley.

1 suckling pig
Salt
Pepper
1 large onion, quartered
1 tablespoon caraway seeds
12 TO 15 SERVINGS *4-inch piece of salt pork*

Rub the cleaned pig on the inside with salt and pepper. Scatter the onion pieces and caraway seeds inside the pig. Rub the outside with the salt pork about every 15 minutes during the roasting. Place the prepared pig on a large pan or broiler tray and roast in a slow oven (325° F.) for 4 to 5 hours, or until the meat is tender throughout. The skin should be evenly browned and crisp. If the ears and snout brown too rapidly, cover them with heavy paper.

BREAST OF VEAL WITH WINE

BORBAN SÜLT BORJÚSZEGY

6 SERVINGS

3 pounds breast of veal
1 teaspoon salt
¼ cup bacon fat
1 cup wine, or more as needed

Lightly score the surface of the veal in 2-inch squares. Sprinkle salt over all. Brown on both sides in the fat. Pour wine over the meat, cover, and simmer slowly until tender, about 1½ hours. If additional wine is necessary to prevent dryness, add it in small quantities.

BREAST OF VEAL WITH LEMON SAUCE

CITROMOS BORJÚSZEGY

6 SERVINGS

2 pounds breast of veal, cut in 2-inch pieces
2 tablespoons finely chopped parsley
1 teaspoon salt
3 tablespoons fat
2 tablespoons flour
2 egg yolks
2 tablespoons lemon juice
⅔ cup rice, steamed

Sprinkle the meat with the parsley and salt; brown in the fat. Add about ¼ cup of water, cover, and slowly cook until tender, about 1 hour. Occasionally add a few spoonfuls of water, if the meat becomes dry—it should not roast. Dust with the flour, stir it in, then thin the gravy with ½ cup of water. Remove the meat to a hot platter. Mix the egg yolks with the lemon juice, and stir into the gravy. Heat gently for a minute, then pour around the meat. Serve with the steamed rice.

VEAL CHOPS WITH CREAMED MUSHROOMS

BORJÚSZELET GOMBAKRÉMMEL

8 SERVINGS

8 veal chops
1 teaspoon salt
2 tablespoons fat
½ pound mushrooms, sliced
2 tablespoons butter
2 tablespoons chopped parsley
1 small clove garlic, chopped
½ cup sour cream

Salt the chops and brown on each side in the fat. Place in a baking dish. Brown the mushrooms in the butter with the parsley and garlic. Stir in the sour cream. Mix well and pour over the chops. Bake in a slow oven (325° F.), for 1 hour, or until the veal is tender.

VEAL FRICASSEE

BORJÚBECSINÁLT

6 SERVINGS

3 pounds breast of veal, cut in 2-inch pieces
3 tablespoons butter
1 teaspoon salt
⅛ teaspoon pepper
2 carrots, sliced in rings
½ cauliflower, broken into flowerets
¼ pound mushrooms, sliced
2 tablespoons flour
1 tablespoon lemon juice
½ cup water

Brown the veal lightly in the butter. Sprinkle with the salt and pepper; cover and cook slowly for 30 minutes. (Add a few tablespoons of water if meat becomes dry.) Add vegetables and mushrooms, and continue cooking until all are tender. Sprinkle with the flour, and stir it in. When the flour starts to brown, stir in the lemon juice and ½ cup of water. Stir until mixture boils.

BRAISED VEAL

BORJÚPÖRKÖLT

This richly browned meat dish goes well with potatoes, rice, *tarhonya* (egg barley) or *galuska* (soft noodles).

6 SERVINGS

2 large onions, chopped
4 tablespoons fat
1 tablespoon paprika
3 pounds neck of veal, cubed
1 teaspoon salt

Brown the onions in the fat. Add the paprika, veal, and salt. Brown the meat, cover, and simmer for about an hour or until the meat is tender. Add a few tablespoons of water to prevent overbrowning.

Note: To make Paprika Veal, stir 1 cup sour cream into the above dish 5 minutes before serving.

VEAL SOUFFLÉ

BORJÚFELFUJT

6 SERVINGS

1 pound ground veal
6 eggs, separated
½ teaspoon salt
⅛ teaspoon pepper
½ cup bread crumbs
¼ cup melted butter

Mix together the veal and the egg yolks. Stir in the salt, pepper, bread crumbs, and 1 tablespoon of the butter; combine well. Beat the egg whites until very stiff, and fold into the meat mixture. Pile lightly into a buttered baking dish and bake in a slow oven (325° F.) for 1 hour, or until an inserted knife comes out clean. Pour the rest of the butter over the soufflé and serve at once.

CALVES' TONGUES

BORJÚNYELV

6 TO 8 SERVINGS

4 small fresh calves' tongues
2 teaspoons salt
2 eggs, slightly beaten
1 cup flour
¼ cup fat
Pickled beets
Parsley
Horseradish

Boil the tongues about 1 hour in salted water to cover. When tender, drain, plunge into cold water, and peel off the skins. Slice diagonally ¼ inch thick. Dip each slice in egg and coat with flour. Brown lightly in the fat. Arrange the slices on a warm platter and garnish with the beets and parsley. Serve with horseradish.

TRANSYLVANIAN VEAL STEW

BORJÚTOKÁNY

What *gulyás* (goulash) is to the people of the lowlands of Hungary, *tokány* (stew) is to the Transylvanians. The difference lies in the use of black pepper instead of paprika.

¼ cup fat
2 pounds veal, cut in 2-inch pieces
½ teaspoon salt
½ teaspoon pepper
1 cup shredded onions

4 SERVINGS

Heat the fat, add meat, salt, and pepper. Then cover and steam slowly until the meat is nearly tender and quite dry. Stir in the onions, cover again, and cook with the meat until both are tender and beginning to brown. If they start to brown before becoming tender, add ½ cup of water. The meat should remain moist and be only lightly browned.

BANDIT GRILL

ZSIVÁNYPECSENYE

6 SERVINGS

1 pound beef round, sliced ½ inch thick
1 pound veal steak, sliced ½ inch thick
12 slices salt pork, ⅛ inch thick

Cut the beef into 12 pieces and pound each into a flat fillet. Cut the veal into the same number of pieces. Thread alternate pieces of beef, veal, and salt pork onto 6 skewers. Grill over an open fire or under medium-hot broiler, turning frequently. Veal and pork must be well done.

BANDIT ROAST

RABLÓPECSENYE

1 pound beef round, ½ inch thick
1 pound fresh pork steak, ½ inch thick
1 pound veal steak, ½ inch thick
1½ teaspoons salt
3 slices bacon

2 tablespoons fat
6 onions, finely chopped
½ cup vinegar
½ cup water
1 tablespoon sugar

8 SERVINGS

Rub the meat with salt. Using a mallet, pound each piece as thin as possible without tearing. On the beef, place the pork, and on it the veal. Roll up tightly into a cylinder and tie with string. Wrap bacon around the roll. Heat fat in a deep pan, and place the meat roll in it. Add the onion and pour the vinegar and water over all. Cover and cook until the meat is tender and the liquid is gone. Stir in the sugar, and continue cooking until the meat is browned—it must not scorch. Remove string, and cut roll of meat into rounds for individual portions.

BRAISED BEEF

MARHAPÖRKÖLT

2 large onions, chopped
2 tablespoons bacon fat
2 pounds beef chuck or round steak, cut in 2-inch pieces
½ pound liver, cubed
½ pound heart, cubed
2 tablespoons paprika
1½ teaspoons salt
Pinched Noodles

8 SERVINGS

Brown the onions in the fat until golden. Add the meat, paprika, and salt, and brown well. Cover and simmer over low heat until tender, adding about ½ cup of water whenever the meat cooks dry. Serve with Pinched Noodles.

BRAISED CALF'S LIVER

PIRITOTT BORJÚMÁJ

6 SERVINGS

2 pounds calf's liver
1 cup finely chopped onions
¼ cup bacon fat
1 tablespoon paprika
1 tablespoon tomato paste
½ teaspoon salt

Wash the liver, remove veins and membrane. Slice in thin, small pieces. Brown the onions in fat. Stir in the paprika and tomato paste. Add the liver. Cover and simmer over a low flame for 15 minutes, or until the liver is done. Add salt just before serving.

BRAISED RABBIT

NYÚLPÖRKÖLT

Have a rabbit cut into serving-size pieces, and use it in place of liver in the preceding recipe. As rabbit must be cooked longer to become tender, allow 35 minutes.

OXTAIL RAGOUT

ÖKÖRFAROK RAGÚ

Hungarians are fond of oxtail and they prepare it in several ways. This dish is especially attractive with the individual groups of vegetables served around the meat.

2 oxtails, disjointed
¼ cup flour
1 teaspoon salt
2 tablespoons fat

1 large onion, chopped
1 clove garlic, chopped
1 teaspoon paprika
2 ripe tomatoes or 1 cup canned tomatoes
12 scallions, diced, or 12 tiny white onions
12 large mushrooms
12 small carrot balls
1 cup potato balls

6 SERVINGS

Coat the oxtail pieces with flour, sprinkle with the salt, and brown in a large skillet in the hot fat. Stir in the chopped onion, garlic, paprika, and tomatoes. Cover and simmer until meat is tender, about 2 hours. Add 2 tablespoons of water, as needed, to prevent sticking. Around the meat, arrange the rest of the vegetables, keeping each kind in its own section. Make sure there is about ¼ cup of liquid in the skillet. Cover and cook 30 minutes, or until the vegetables are tender.

SOUR TRIPE

SAVANYÚ PACAL

1½ pounds fresh tripe
¾ teaspoon salt
2 tablespoons flour
2 tablespoons butter
1½ cups meat stock
¼ teaspoon pepper
2 egg yolks, slightly beaten
1 tablespoon lemon juice or vinegar

6 SERVINGS

Wash the tripe, and simmer in salted water for 1 hour or longer. Drain, and cut tripe into narrow noodle-like strips. Blend flour and butter; stir the meat stock into it, and cook until thickened and smooth, stirring constantly. Blend in the pepper, egg yolks, and lemon juice. Add the tripe, and heat for 5 or 10 minutes.

SEARED TRIPE

PACALPÖRKÖLT

1½ pounds fresh tripe
2 tablespoons fat
1 onion, finely chopped
1 tablespoon paprika
½ cup white wine
Egg Barley

6 SERVINGS

Cook the tripe as in the preceeding recipe and cut into strips. Brown the onion in the fat. Add paprika and tripe. Pour over wine, heat for 10 minutes. Serve with Egg Barley.

SOUR OXTAIL RAGOUT

SAVANYÚ ÖKÖRFAROK

2 oxtails, disjointed
½ cup vinegar
1 onion
1 carrot
1 clove garlic
Rind of 1 lemon
2 bay leaves
2 cloves
6 peppercorns
½ teaspoon salt
2 tablespoons flour
2 tablespoons fat
¼ cup sour cream

6 SERVINGS

Combine the oxtails, vinegar, vegetables, and seasonings. Cover with boiling water and cook until the meat is tender and loosening from bones. Add water as needed to keep about 1 cup of liquid. Blend the flour and fat over low heat. Strain into this mixture the liquid from the meat. Stir and cook until thickened and smooth. Add the oxtail pieces. Before serving, stir in the sour cream.

SOUR OXTAIL WITH POTATO DUMPLINGS

SAVANYÚ ÖKÖRFAROK GOMBÓCCAL

This is a favorite supper dish. With the dumplings it makes a substantial meal.

1 oxtail, disjointed
3 cups water
2 tablespoons vinegar
1 onion
1 bay leaf
1 teaspoon salt
6 peppercorns
2 tablespoons flour
2 tablespoons fat
¼ cup sour cream
Potato Dumplings

4 SERVINGS

Simmer the oxtail in the water with vinegar, onion, bay leaf, salt, and peppercorns. Cover the kettle and add water as needed to prevent scorching. When the meat begins to loosen from the bones, lift it out. Add enough water to the meat broth to make about 1½ cups. Blend the flour and fat; stir the meat broth into the mixture and cook until smooth and thickened. Replace the meat, and simmer for 10 minutes. Stir in the sour cream, and serve with the freshly cooked dumplings.

POULTRY

POULTRY

The famous French gourmet, Brillat-Savarin, in *The Physiology of Taste*, says: ". . . poultry is, for the cook, what canvas is for the painter. . . ." The artistry of Hungarian cooks with chicken is unexcelled. Their boned stuffed chicken, sliced cold, is one of the choicest of chicken dishes. Much better known is the paprika treatment of chicken. *Pörkölt csirke* (braised chicken), without cream but rich with sweet paprika, and *paprikás csirke* (paprika chicken) with sour cream are dishes fit for the gods—both at home and abroad. Breaded chicken is another specialty.

The holidays or events of the moment find a large chicken, capon, or young goose stuffed or roasted on festive tables. In Hungary as in other countries, the turkey—the New World's gift to the Old—is highly regarded, and on feast days those who can afford it serve roast turkey stuffed with chestnut dressing.

Hungarian geese are famous the world over for the delicacies that are made from their enormous livers. The export of goose liver to France, England, the United States, and other countries was once a thriving business. Goose fat as well as chicken fat plays an important role in Hungarian kitchens. Lard is the only fat more generally used.

BOILED STUFFED CHICKEN

FŐTT TÖLTÖTT CSIRKE

This chicken, which takes some little effort to prepare, is most delicious—wonderful for a party. It's the crowning glory at a cold buffet.

4½-pound roasting chicken
2 teaspoons salt
1 onion, finely chopped
2 tablespoons butter
1 pound ground veal
½ pound chicken livers, scraped free of membrane
1 large baker's roll, soaked in milk and pressed dry
2 hard-cooked eggs
2 fresh tomatoes
1 tablespoon paprika
2 raw eggs
¼ cup sour cream
Salt
2 cloves garlic
1 carrot, sliced
3 tablespoons chopped parsley
6 sprigs parsley
Lemon slices
Radishes

8 TO 10 SERVINGS

Have the chicken cleaned and boned by the butcher. (Some merchants will do this for an extra charge.) He should leave only the leg and wing bones. The meat should not be torn. Rub chicken all over with salt.

Wilt the onion in the butter. Add the veal and chicken livers.

Press excess moisture from the roll and force it through a strainer, along with the cooked eggs and the tomatoes. Combine with the meat, paprika, raw eggs, sour cream, and salt. Mix well. Stuff the chicken with mixture. Sew all openings. Tie up in a buttered napkin, and place in a large kettle with water to cover.

Add garlic, carrot, and chopped parsley. Cook slowly for 1½ hours, or until the chicken is tender. It should not be overcooked. Remove carefully to a platter. Chill overnight. Remove the wings. Garnish the rest with the remaining parsley, lemon slices, and radishes. Slice the chicken crosswise and serve.

BOILED STUFFED TURKEY

FŐTT TÖLTÖTT PULYKA

Use ground pork or ham instead of the chicken livers in the preceding recipe. Include a calf's brain and ½ pound of mushrooms, cooked and ground. Season the stuffing with a small amount of black pepper instead of the paprika. Add the grated rind of a lemon. Mix the stuffing and proceed as for Boiled Stuffed Chicken.

Note: Boned capon is good with either stuffing.

CHICKEN WITH CABBAGE

KÁPOSZTÁS CSIRKE

The combination of chicken and cabbage seems strange in America but it is a familiar one in Hungary. It is used to give variety on tables where chicken belongs to everyday fare.

3½-pound chicken, disjointed
1 cup white wine
1½ teaspoons salt
1 onion, finely chopped
½ head cabbage, chopped
3 tablespoons fat
½ teaspoon pepper
1 tablespoon lemon juice

8 SERVINGS

Wash the chicken. Simmer in a covered kettle with the wine and salt until tender, about 1 hour. Brown the onion and cabbage in the fat. Add the pepper, lemon juice, and then the chicken. Cover tightly, and steam all together for 15 minutes.

BREADED CHICKEN

RÁNTOTT CSIRKE

This is a favorite Sunday-dinner dish in Hungary, served often when chickens are young.

3-pound frying chicken, disjointed
1 teaspoon salt
¼ cup flour
2 eggs, slightly beaten
1 cup fine bread crumbs
½ cup fat

6 SERVINGS

Wash the chicken well, and dry on a towel. Sprinkle with salt. Pour the flour into a large paper bag. Put in the pieces of chicken and shake. Tear open the bag, and dip the individual pieces first in the egg, then in the crumbs. The coating should be light. Heat the fat in a large skillet. Add the chicken, and fry slowly until golden on one side, then on the other. Turn the heat ouite low during the last of the cooking.

CHOPPED CHICKEN BREAST

VAGDALT CSIRKEMELL

This is a choice entree used for a light meal. It is a specialty often prepared for convalescents.

1-pound cooked chicken breast
1 small onion, browned in butter
1 tablespoon chopped parsley
1 baker's roll or 2 slices bread
½ cup milk
½ teaspoon salt
3 eggs, separated
2 cups hot fat

4 SERVINGS

Put the chicken and onion through a grinder. Add the parsley. Moisten the roll or bread in the milk. Add the salt and egg yolks. Combine with the chicken mixture and blend. Beat the egg whites stiff and fold into the chicken mixture. Drop into the hot fat by tablespoons. Fry until golden brown on each side.

Note: Turkey breast may also be prepared in this manner. Other than breast meat may be used, from either chicken or turkey, but the result is not so delicate.

CHICKEN WITH RAISINS À LA DEBRECZEN

DEBRECZENI MAZSOLÁS CSIRKE

This is a traditional dish at weddings in Debreczen. It is served as the main dinner course. Quantities of other meats, fruits, cakes, and barrels of homemade wine will be lavishly offered, but a wedding feast is seldom planned without this special chicken.

4-pound chicken, disjointed
2 teaspoons salt
1 lemon, thinly sliced
½ cup vinegar
½ cup water
½ cup raisins
½ cup sugar
1 cup wine
2 tablespoons flour
3 tablespoons fat

8 SERVINGS

Wash the chicken well. Cover with the boiling, salted water, and cook slowly until tender, about 2 hours. Combine the lemon slices, vinegar, and the ½ cup of water, and cook 30 minutes. Drain. Combine the raisins, sugar, and wine, and cook until the raisins are plump. When the chicken is done and most of the liquid has cooked away, add the lemon slices. Blend the flour and fat over low heat. Stir in a cup of the chicken broth and continue cooking and stirring until mixture is smooth and thickened. Add the raisins in wine, and blend. Arrange the chicken on a platter and pour the sauce over it.

PAPRIKA CHICKEN

PAPRIKÁSCSIRKE

This is a favorite dish for dinner or supper. Its popularity in the United States is almost as great as in Hungary.

3-pound frying chicken, disjointed
2 onions, finely chopped
3 tablespoons fat
1 tablespoon paprika
1 teaspoon salt
1 cup sour cream
Soft noodles

6 SERVINGS

Wash the chicken well and drain. Brown the onion lightly in the fat; add the paprika and the chicken. Sprinkle with salt. Cover and cook slowly about 1 hour or until tender. Pour the cream over chicken. Heat for a minute only. Serve with freshly boiled soft noodles.

SEARED CHICKEN

PÖRKÖLTCSIRKE

Prepare as for Paprika Chicken but omit sour cream.

CHICKEN WITH MUSTARD

MUSTÁROS CSIRKE

4-pound chicken, stewed
Prepared mustard
2 tablespoons butter
2 tablespoons flour
1 cup heavy cream
¼ teaspoon salt

6 SERVINGS

Remove the cooked chicken from the bones, in large pieces. Arrange in a baking dish, and spread thinly with the mustard. Blend the butter and flour; add the cream and salt, and mix. Pour over the chicken, and bake in a moderate oven (350° F.) for 20 minutes.

CHICKEN WITH MAYONNAISE SAUCE

MAJONÉZES CSIRKE

8 SERVINGS

4-pound fowl, disjointed
2 teaspoons salt
1 cup mayonnaise
1 tablespoon prepared mustard
1 teaspoon sugar
1/8 teaspoon paprika
1/4 cup sour cream
1 tablespoon lemon juice
1 hard-cooked egg, sliced
1 pickled beet, sliced
1 cucumber, sliced

Cook the fowl in boiling, salted water to cover about 1 1/2 hours, or until tender. Meanwhile blend the mayonnaise, mustard, sugar, paprika, cream and lemon juice. Remove the skin from the chicken and lift the meat from the bones, in large pieces. Cool and arrange the meat on a serving platter and cover with the mayonnaise mixture. Garnish with the egg, beet, and cucumber slices.

ROAST CHICKEN WITH MUSHROOM STUFFING

GOMBÁVAL TÖLTÖTT SÜLT CSIRKE

5-pound roasting chicken
1/2 pound mushrooms, chopped

¼ cup butter
3 large baker's rolls or 6 slices bread moistened in milk
Giblets, cooked and chopped
2 hard-cooked eggs, chopped
1 raw egg
½ teaspoon salt
⅛ teaspoon pepper

8 SERVINGS

Rub the chicken with salt inside and out. Brown the mushrooms in the butter. Combine with the softened bread, giblets, cooked and raw eggs, ½ teaspoon salt, and the pepper. Stuff the chicken loosely. Sew up openings and roast in an open pan in a slow oven (300° F.) for 2½ hours, or until chicken is tender. Baste the chicken with the drippings every half hour while roasting. If necessary, increase heat a little toward the end to brown the bird.

ROAST YOUNG GOOSE

FIATAL SÜLT LIBA

Roast goose is a special delicacy in Hungary, in the spring when the fowl is young. The whole baker's rolls placed within the goose are not intended as stuffing but are meant to absorb excess fat.

8-pound goose
1 teaspoon marjoram
3 teaspoons salt
1 teaspoon pepper
2 baker's rolls
Small piece of salt pork

6 TO 8 SERVINGS

Rub the goose with marjoram on the inside, with salt and pepper on the outside. Place the whole rolls within the bird. Pierce the skin in several places to allow fat to ooze out. Roast in a slow oven (325° F.) for about 3½ hours, or until tender. Baste with drippings four times during the first hour. Rub with salt pork several times during the rest of the cooking period. The skin should become crisp. Serve very hot with Cucumbers with Sour Cream.

FRICASSEE OF GOOSE GIBLETS

BECSINÁLT LIBAAPRÓLÉK

This dish is beloved by young and old. It is prepared for the family—not for guests.

Goose giblets, head, neck, and wings
5 peppercorns
1 sprig parsley, chopped
2 stalks celery, chopped
1 onion, chopped
1 tomato, peeled and diced
2 tablespoons flour
3 tablespoons cold water
Juice of ½ lemon
4 cups freshly steamed rice

6 SERVINGS

Simmer giblets, head, neck, and wings in boiling salted water to cover, until nearly tender, about 1 hour. Remove the liver and heart after 10 minutes. Add the seasonings and vegetables, and continue cooking until meat loosens from bones. Blend the flour and cold water. Add the lemon juice. Dilute with the meat broth and simmer 5 minutes. Combine with the giblets, meat, and vegetables. Serve over the steaming rice.

PARTRIDGE WITH SAVOY CABBAGE

FOGOLY KELKÁPOSZTÁVAL

During hunting season this dish is popular for stag dinners. It is prepared with skill and pride of accomplishment.

3 whole partridges
Salt
3 tablespoons fat
3 heads savoy cabbage
Boiling salted water
2 cups sour or sweet cream
4 cups freshly steamed rice

6 SERVINGS

Clean the birds and fold under the wings. Split through the breast and back. Rub with salt and the fat. Roast in hot oven

(400° F.) for 15 minutes. Core the cabbage and cook in the boiling salted water only until wilted. Cut in half, and drain well. Remove as many inside leaves of each cabbage half as necessary to make room for half a partridge. Fit half a bird into each cavity. Bind two halves together with string and place in a roasting pan. Roast in a moderate oven (350° F.) for 1 hour, or until the cabbage and the partridge meat are tender. Baste frequently with the cream during the roasting.

To serve, remove the string and open up each cabbage but do not remove the bird from the cabbage nests. Arrange on plates of freshly steamed rice, and serve with the cream drippings from the roasting pan.

FISH

FISH

Hungary is a country with no outlet to the sea. Fiume, once its only seaport, now belongs to Italy. The prejudice of the Hungarian people against fish brought from a distance makes salt-water fish almost unknown in Magyar kitchens. The Tisza and Danube rivers and Lake Balaton richly compensate, however, with abundant supplies of fresh-water fish.

Excellent *kecsege* (sturgeon) from the rivers is appreciated for its tender white meat and lack of small bones. The roe of this splended fish gives fine-quality caviar. Lake Balaton produces the *fogas*, considered by gourmets the most excellent of all fish. It has tender, snow-white flesh, and is free from small bones. Many other countries, which import the *fogas*, prize it highly and recognize its incomparable quality.

Trout from the lakes is also excellent. But even more popular are the less expensive *silure* or catfish, perch, pike, and carp. They are boiled, steamed, broiled, baked, and fried with bread crumbs; served hot or cold, marinated or jellied. Many families would go hungry, were it not for the plentiful supply of fish.

BAKED FISH WITH RICE

HARCSA RIZZSEL

½ cup rice
1 large onion, chopped
4 tablespoons fat
2 pounds fish steaks
½ teaspoon salt
1 tablespoon paprika

6 SERVINGS

Cook the rice in boiling, salted water until done. Meanwhile fry the onion in the fat until lightly browned. Stir in the cooked rice, and arrange the fish on it. Sprinkle with the salt and paprika. Bake in a moderately hot oven (375° F.) for 15 minutes. Turn the fish and bake 15 minutes longer.

BOILED STURGEON

KECSEGE VAJJAL

A bachelor in Hungary, inviting a small party for after-theater supper, might serve this fish, cold. Small baskets made from ½ lemon (with the fruit pulp scooped out) would be filled with caviar. These baskets and hard-cooked eggs make a beautiful garnish for the tender white fish. Small buttered rolls would be eaten with the caviar.

1 carrot, sliced
1 onion, sliced
1 knob celery, sliced
1 sprig parsley
2 bay leaves
5 peppercorns
¼ cup vinegar
1½ pounds sturgeon
2 tablespoons melted butter

4 SERVINGS

Put the vegetables, seasonings, and vinegar into a kettle of boiling water. Tie the fish up in a piece of cheesecloth about 18 inches square, and lower it into the kettle. Simmer gently for 15 minutes, or until fish seems tender when pierced with a fork through the cheesecloth.

Lift out the cloth bag, untie, and roll the fish onto a warm platter. Remove the bones and season with the butter.

PIKE POACHED IN MILK

TEJBENFŐTT HAL

4 SERVINGS

1 large pike
2 cups milk
1 teaspoon salt
3 tablespoons butter
3 tablespoons flour

Clean the fish and remove head and tail. Poach in the milk, with salt, until fish is tender, about 10 minutes. Place on a warm platter. Blend the butter and flour, stir into it the hot milk, and heat slowly until thickened and smooth. Pour sauce over the fish and serve.

WHITE FISH BAKED IN WHITE WINE

SÜLT HAL FEHÉRBORBAN

6 SERVINGS

3 medium-size potatoes, thinly sliced
2 tablespoons butter
1 cup sour cream
½ pound (2 cups) sliced mushrooms
⅔ cup white wine
2 pounds fish fillets, cut into servings
1 teaspoon salt

Line a buttered baking dish with the potato slices. Dot with butter and pour over about half of the cream. Cook mushrooms in the wine for 10 minutes, then add to the potatoes. Arrange pieces of fish over all; sprinkle with the salt, and top with remaining cream. Bake in a moderate oven (350° F.) for about 30 minutes, or until potatoes are done.

FISH IN WINE

BORBANFŐTT HAL

1 carrot, sliced
1 knob celery, sliced
1 kohlrabi, diced
1 onion, sliced
1 sprig parsley, chopped
2 tablespoons butter
2 pounds fish
1 cup white wine
1 teaspoon salt
1/8 teaspoon pepper

6 SERVINGS

Simmer the vegetables, covered, in the butter until nearly done. Cut the fish in serving pieces and arrange over the vegetables. Pour on the wine, sprinkle with salt and pepper, cover, and cook over low heat until the fish is tender and the sauce becomes slightly thickened, about 15 minutes.

FOGAS OR HALIBUT WITH TARTARE SAUCE

FOGAS TATÁRMÁRTÁSSAL

Fogas, the "king" of Lake Balaton, is excellent served cold with tartare sauce. Any fine white fish, such as young cod or halibut, may be used.

2 pounds fish steaks
1 teaspoon salt
2 hard-cooked eggs
Tartare sauce

4 SERVINGS

Cook fish in salted water to cover, for 15 minutes. Leave in the liquid until cold. Carefully remove the flesh from the bones and arrange on a platter. Garnish with hard-cooked eggs, and serve with tartare sauce.

JELLIED PAPRIKA FISH

PAPRIKÁS HALKOCSONYA

2 pounds whole fish with heads
2 extra fish heads
2 onions, finely chopped
2 tablespoons fat
½ teaspoon salt
1 tablespoon paprika

6 SERVINGS

Clean the fish, including the heads. Stir the onions in the hot fat until golden, then add the paprika. Put the salted fish in this sauce. Cover with water and cook slowly until fish is tender, about 30 minutes. Remove and bone the fish. Arrange the flesh in a jelly mold or loaf pan, and return the bones to the hot liquid. Cook 10 minutes longer; then strain over the fish. Chill in the refrigerator until jellied. Serve cold.

PIKE BAKED IN CREAM

TÉPETT CSUKA

2 pounds pike fillets
½ teaspoon salt
½ cup bread crumbs
1 cup sour cream

6 SERVINGS

Arrange a layer of fish in a buttered dish; sprinkle with salt and crumbs and spread with cream. Repeat layers until all is used. Bake in a slow oven (325° F.) for 30 minutes, or until fish is tender. Serve in baking dish.

PIKE WITH CREAM AND HORSERADISH

CSUKA TEJFELESEN TORMÁVAL

6 SERVINGS

1 carrot, sliced
1 onion, chopped
1 tablespoon chopped parsley
2 cups water
½ teaspoon salt
1 tablespoon butter
2 tablespoons flour
1 cup heavy sweet or sour cream
2 pounds pike fillets
2 tablespoons freshly grated horseradish

Cook the vegetables in the water until they are soft. Remove, and strain liquid. Blend the salt, butter, and flour; add the cream, then stir in the liquid strained from the vegetables. Return to the heat and stir the sauce until it comes to a boil. Add the fish, and simmer for 20 minutes, or until fish is tender. Remove the fish to a warm platter; spread with horseradish, and pour the sauce over it. Serve at once.

FISH WITH SAUERKRAUT

HARCSÁS KÁPOSZTA

1 onion, chopped
2 tablespoons bacon fat

1 tablespoon paprika
1 pound (2 cups) sauerkraut
2 pounds fish fillets
½ cup sour cream

6 SERVINGS

Brown the onions in bacon fat. Stir in the paprika and then the sauerkraut, and cook slowly for 1 hour. Cut the fish into 6 serving-size pieces; stir the sauerkraut, then arrange the fish on top of it. Cover, and cook slowly for 45 minutes longer. Before serving, spoon the sour cream onto the fish pieces, and cover for 2 minutes to heat the cream.

Variation: The sauerkraut may be cooked alone, the fish browned in the fat and paprika, and then carefully arranged over the sauerkraut. A cup of heavy sweet cream may be used instead of the sour cream. It should also be covered long enough to heat.

SERBIAN CARP

RÁCPONTY

2 large carp, cleaned and split
¼ cup butter, or 4 slices bacon
4 potatoes, pared and thinly sliced
2 tablespoons paprika
2 tablespoons flour
1 teaspoon salt
1 cup heavy sweet cream

6 SERVINGS

Make diagonal cuts on the skin side of the fish. Fill the cuts with butter, or cover them with bacon strips. Arrange the fish on a rack in a shallow baking pan. Under the rack spread the potato slices. Mix the paprika, flour, and salt, and sprinkle over the fish. Bake in a moderately hot oven (375° F.) for about 40 minutes, or until fish and potatoes are tender. When the skin of the fish starts to shrink, baste with cream and repeat as needed.

Note: Sturgeon is equally good prepared in this manner.

STUFFED PERCH

SÜLLŐ TÖLTVE

2-pound perch
½ cup bread crumbs
4 anchovies, chopped
1 onion, finely chopped
1 teaspoon chopped parsley
1 tablespoon paprika
4 tablespoons butter
Lemon slices

4 SERVINGS

Clean and bone the fish. Combine the crumbs, anchovies, onion, parsley, and half the paprika and butter. Stuff the fish with this mixture. Place in a buttered baking dish. Rub the outside of the fish with the remaining butter, and sprinkle with the paprika. Bake in moderately hot oven (375° F.) for about 30 minutes, or until fish is tender. Garnish with lemon.

TROUT WITH MAYONNAISE

MAJONÉZES PISZTRÁNG

2 cups water
½ cup wine vinegar
1 onion, sliced
3 peppercorns
1 bay leaf

½ teaspoon salt
½ teaspoon sugar
2 medium-size trout, cleaned
Radishes
Parsley
Mayonnaise

4 SERVINGS

Combine the water, vinegar, onion, and seasonings, and bring to a boil. Carefully place fish in the hot liquid and simmer gently for 10 minutes. Cool the fish in the liquid, then remove to a warm platter. Garnish with radishes and parsley. Serve with mayonnaise.

VEGETABLES

VEGETABLES

Hungarians take no part of their food program lightly, and their devotion to cookery is evident even in their concern over their vegetable dishes. The simply prepared boiled vegetables topped with butter are "for the sick" or for those on a diet. So uncommon are they on Hungarian tables that this school of cookery is called *à l'anglaise* (English style). A richer form of preparation is more popular at the Hungarian table. An example of this is the dish consisting of layers of cooked vegetables arranged in a deep casserole with a covering of butter, sour cream, and bread crumbs. This is then heated in the oven until the top crumbs are brown.

Regarded with greatest approbation are the vegetable dishes prepared with thickening or cream—especially sour cream—and seasoned with paprika, dill, a little lemon juice or vinegar, or onions. It is interesting to discover the similarity between the seasonings and accents used in Hungarian vegetable dishes and those used in the soups. The difference is in the "length" or thickness of the gravy. Instead of serving vegetables with a cream sauce as is customary in many American kitchens, Hungarian cooks often thicken their vegetables by "dusting" flour onto the cooked, drained vegetables, tossing the two together, then adding the liquid that has been removed. Or they may combine that liquid with meat broth, cream, or milk. When this comes to a boil, the sauce is made.

Hungarians miss their native-type vegetables when traveling in foreign lands. They dream longingly of the "thickened" creations of their excellent kitchens. As in many countries, the vegetable is considered by the Hungarians as only the beginning of a delightful dish to which must be added exciting seasonings and flavors. It has little appeal for its own flavor.

Stuffed vegetables are popular. These are usually prepared with a filling of meat and rice. Though cabbage is the favorite stuffed vegetable, green peppers, kohlrabi, tomatoes, cucumbers, and squash are also prepared with meat stuffing. Both the stuffed and the thickened vegetable make a substantial part of the meal. In rural Hungary as in rural America, the tendency is to find substance and nourishment without unduly straining the food budget.

Good summer vegetables grow in profusion throughout Hungary and are widely used in season. The new potato, always a treat after the long winter of eating stored potatoes, is extremely important to the Hungarian household. Other spring and summer favorites are fresh peas, squash, green beans, cabbage, kohlrabi, spinach, sorrel, carrots, sweet green peppers, lettuce, cucumbers, tomatoes, and cauliflower.

In season all of these are to be found in the markets, but in winter the cities and villages and farms have only the vegetables that store and can well.

DRIED BEANS WITH SOUR CREAM

SZÁRITOTT BABFŐZELÉK

1½ cups dried white beans
2 teaspoons salt
1 onion, finely chopped
2 tablespoons fat
2 tablespoons flour
1 tablespoon vinegar
½ cup sour cream

6 SERVINGS

Soak the beans overnight in cold water. Drain, cover with fresh water, add salt, and cook slowly 2 to 3 hours, or until tender. Brown the onion in the fat; blend in the flour. Add the vinegar and about a cup of water to make a fairly thick sauce. Drain the beans and combine with the sauce. Just before serving, stir in the cream.

STRING BEANS

ZÖLDBABFŐZELÉK

An especially delicious variation for green or wax beans.

1½ pounds green beans
1½ cups boiling water
½ teaspoon salt
6 strips bacon, chopped
1 onion, finely chopped
2 tablespoons flour
1 tablespoon vinegar
⅔ cup sour cream

6 SERVINGS

String the beans and cut off the ends. Break into 1-inch lengths. Put into the water, add salt, and cover the kettle. Boil about 35 minutes, or until the beans are tender. Brown the bacon, add the onion, and fry slightly. Stir in the flour, then the vinegar and the liquid from the cooked beans. Cook until smooth and creamy. Combine with the beans. Stir in cream and cover for 2 minutes to heat before serving.

STRING BEANS BAKED WITH CREAM

TEJFELES ZÖLDBAB

6 SERVINGS

1½ pounds string beans
½ teaspoon salt
1 tablespoon butter
½ cup heavy sweet or sour cream
¼ cup bread crumbs

Remove ends and strings from the beans. Heat a small amount of water to boiling, add the salt and the uncut beans. Cover and cook until the beans are tender, about 35 minutes. Drain and arrange in a baking dish. Dot with the butter, pour in the cream, and top with the crumbs. Brown in a moderately hot oven (375° F.) for 10 minutes.

RED CABBAGE

VÖRÖS KÁPOSZTA

6 SERVINGS

1 head red cabbage, thinly sliced
1 teaspoon salt
2 tablespoons fat
2 tablespoons sugar
½ cup white wine
2 tart apples, pared and sliced

Simmer salted cabbage in fat. Add sugar and wine. Simmer 10 minutes longer. Add the apple slices and, if needed, 2 or 3 more tablespoons of wine. Cook until cabbage and apples are tender.

SAVOY CABBAGE WITH CHESTNUTS

KELKÁPOSZTA GESZTENYÉVEL

An interesting combination of flavors and textures results when cabbage and chestnuts are combined.

6 SERVINGS

1 head savoy cabbage
½ teaspoon salt
2 cups boiling water
½ pound chestnuts, cooked and peeled
2 tablespoons butter
2 tablespoons flour

Cut the cabbage into small sections. Cook, with the salt, in the boiling water until tender. Drain, but reserve the cooking water. Slice the chestnuts and mix with the cabbage. Melt the butter, add the flour, then stir in the water drained from the cabbage. Stir until mixture comes to a boil and is a smooth sauce. Combine with the cabbage and chestnuts. Cook for 10 minutes longer.

SAVOY CABBAGE WITH POTATOES

KELKÁPOSZTA BURGONYÁVAL

8 SERVINGS

4 medium-size potatoes
1 head savoy cabbage
2 tablespoons flour
2 tablespoons fat
⅛ teaspoon pepper

Cut the cabbage into small chunks, and cook it in boiling salted water for 15 minutes. Pare and cube potatoes; add to cabbage and cook until tender. Lightly brown the flour in the fat. Add the pepper and enough of the water from the cooked cabbage and potatoes to make a medium-thick sauce (about 1½ cups). Stir until mixture boils. Combine with the potatoes and cabbage, and reheat.

STUFFED HEAD OF CABBAGE

TÖLTÖTT KÁPOSZTÁFEJ

6 SERVINGS

1 head cabbage
2 cups cooked meat
1 cup Béchamel Sauce
¼ cup grated cheese

Remove the core from the cabbage. Cook the uncut head in boiling salted water until nearly tender. Drain and scoop out the center. Stuff with the meat. Place in a baking dish, cover with the Béchamel Sauce, and top with the cheese. Bake in a moderately hot oven (375° F.) for 30 minutes.

STUFFED CABBAGE

TÖLTÖTT KÁPOSZTA

This stuffed cabbage is probably the best-known and most loved vegetable dish served in Hungary.

6 cups sauerkraut
12 large, unbroken cabbage leaves
½ cup water
1 onion, chopped
3 tablespoons fat
2 pounds lean, ground pork
1 cup steamed rice
2 eggs

1 teaspoon salt
1 teaspoon paprika
1 cup sour cream

6 SERVINGS

Simmer the sauerkraut for 1 hour in a large covered kettle. Meanwhile steam the cabbage leaves in the water until slightly wilted. Drain and cool. Brown the onion in the fat. Add the pork and brown it. Stir in the rice, eggs, salt, and paprika. Divide this meat mixture onto the cabbage leaves. Roll up and tuck in the ends. Remove half the sauerkraut. Place the cabbage rolls in the kettle upon the other half, then cover with the remaining kraut and simmer for 2 hours. Add cream before serving.

CAULIFLOWER WITH HAM

KARFIOL SONKÁVAL

1 head cauliflower
½ cup chopped cooked ham
½ cup grated cheese
3 egg yolks, slightly beaten
1 tablespoon flour
½ teaspoon salt
1 cup light cream

6 SERVINGS

Break the cauliflower into flowerets and cook in slightly salted water until almost tender. Arrange layers of the cauliflower, ham, and cheese in a buttered baking dish. Reserve some cheese for the top. Blend the egg yolks, flour, salt, and cream, and pour over the layers. Sprinkle the top with cheese. Bake in a slow oven (325° F.) until the egg mixture thickens, about 25 minutes.

CREAMED CUCUMBERS

UBORKA FŐZELÉK

4 TO 6 SERVINGS

4 large cucumbers
1 onion, sliced
½ teaspoon salt
⅛ teaspoon pepper
1 cup meat stock or water
2 tablespoons flour
Juice of 1 lemon
¼ cup sour cream

Split the cucumbers lengthwise and scrape out the seeds. Slice crosswise, combine with the onion, salt, and pepper. Let stand 1 hour. Drain, then cook in the meat stock or water until tender. Blend the flour with the lemon juice and a tablespoon or so of water as needed to make a smooth paste. Add to cucumbers and stir until mixture boils. Stir in the cream and serve immediately.

STUFFED GREEN PEPPERS

TÖLTÖTT ZÖLDPAPRIKA

6 OR MORE SERVINGS

12 green peppers
2 pounds ground pork
½ cup cooked rice
1 teaspoon paprika
2 teaspoons salt
1 egg, slightly beaten
1 onion, finely chopped
2 tablespoons fat
1½ cups strained tomatoes or tomato juice

Remove stems from the peppers and scoop out seeds. Avoid breaking the shells. Combine the pork, rice, paprika, salt, and egg. Brown the onion in the fat, and add to the meat mixture. Pack loosely in the peppers. Arrange in a baking dish and pour in the tomato juice. Cook in a moderately hot oven (375° F.) for 1 hour. The pork should then be well done and the peppers tender, but not broken.

KOHLRABI

KALARÁBÉ FŐZELÉK

4 TO 6 SERVINGS

1 teaspoon sugar
2 tablespoons fat
2 cups cubed kohlrabi
½ teaspoon salt
1 tablespoon flour
½ cup meat stock

Brown the sugar in the fat. Add the kohlrabi and the salt. Cover and cook slowly until tender. A little water may be added as necessary to prevent scorching during the cooking. Sprinkle the flour over the cooked kohlrabi. Stir, then add the meat stock and heat to boiling.

STUFFED LETTUCE

TÖLTÖTT SALÁTA

6 SERVINGS

6 large green lettuce leaves
2 baker's rolls
1 cup milk
¼ pound mushrooms, chopped
4 tablespoons melted butter
1 tablespoon chopped parsley
2 egg yolks
½ teaspoon salt
½ cup sour cream
½ cup chicken stock

Scald the lettuce leaves briefly to wilt them. Soften the rolls in the milk, squeeze out, and press through a strainer. Cook the mushrooms with half the butter, the parsley, and the salt. Combine with the pressed rolls, and add egg yolks and cream. Spread mixture on each lettuce leaf and roll up. Arrange close together in a buttered baking dish, add the chicken stock, and bake in a hot oven (400° F.) for 20 minutes. Remove to a serving dish, pour the remaining butter over the lettuce rolls, and serve.

GREEN PEAS

ZÖLDBORSÓFŐZELÉK

2 pounds fresh peas
½ cup boiling water
½ teaspoon salt
1 teaspoon sugar
2 tablespoons butter
1 tablespoon chopped parsley
2 tablespoons flour
1 cup chicken broth

4 SERVINGS

Combine the peas, water, and salt. Cover and boil 10 minutes. Drain. Brown the sugar in the butter. Add the parsley and the peas, and cook slowly until the peas are tender, about 10 minutes. Stir in the flour, then the chicken broth. Continue stirring until mixture boils.

YELLOW PEAS WITH BACON

SÁRGABORSÓ SZALONNÁVAL

½ cup dried yellow peas
3 cups boiling water
1 teaspoon salt

6 SERVINGS

½ pound bacon
2 tablespoons flour

Cook the peas in boiling salted water until tender, about 2 hours. Fry the bacon slowly until crisp. Remove to absorbent paper and pour off all but 2 tablespoons of the fat. Combine the flour with this. Add the liquid from the peas, and stir over low heat until thickened. Add the peas. Serve topped with the crisp bacon.

POTATO CAKES

BURGONYAPOGÁCSA

6 SERVINGS

6 medium-size potatoes, pared
2 eggs, slightly beaten
2 onions, chopped
3 tablespoons fat
1 cup bread crumbs

Cook the potatoes in boiling salted water until tender. Drain and mash. Add the eggs and mix well. Brown the onions in the fat and mix with the potatoes. Form small cakes, roll in crumbs, and brown lightly on each side in the hot fat.

POTATOES WITH COTTAGE CHEESE

TÚRÓS BURGONYA

6 SERVINGS

5 medium-size potatoes, pared and diced
1 teaspoon salt
1 pound cottage cheese
1 tablespoon butter
½ cup heavy cream

Arrange half of the potatoes in a greased baking dish. Sprinkle with half the salt. Press the cheese through a strainer, letting half of it fall over the first layer of potatoes. Add half the butter and half the cream. Repeat with another layer of potatoes, salt, cheese, butter, and cream. Bake in a moderately hot oven (375° F.) until potatoes are tender, about 1 hour.

POTATO CAKES WITH HAM

SONKÁS BURGONYASZELET

5 medium-size potatoes, pared
1½ teaspoons salt
1 onion, chopped
1 tablespoon bacon fat
1 cup ground ham or leftover meat
1 egg

6 SERVINGS

Cook the potatoes in boiling, salted water until tender. Drain and mash. Brown the onion in the fat. Add the meat and egg, and combine with the potatoes. Shape into round cakes and arrange in a well-greased, shallow pan. Bake in a hot oven (450° F.) for 20 minutes.

LAYER POTATOES

RAKOTT BURGONYA

6 medium-size potatoes
3 hard-cooked eggs
1 teaspoon salt
1 cup sour cream
½ cup chopped boiled ham
½ cup bread crumbs
2 tablespoons melted butter
½ cup heavy cream

6 TO 8 SERVINGS

Cook the potatoes in boiling water. Pare and slice. Arrange a third of the slices in a greased baking dish. Over these slice the eggs and sprinkle with the salt. Cover with half the sour cream. Make another layer of potato slices, then one of ham, covered with the rest of the cream and a final layer of potatoes. Top with the crumbs mixed with the butter. Add the cream. Bake in a hot oven (450° F.) for 30 minutes, or until crumbs brown.

SUMMER SQUASH

TÖKFŐZELÉK

The Hungarian summer squash resembles the watermelon in shape and is pale green. Hungarian families, rich and poor, use wooden slicing boards for cutting their squash into strips.

1 summer squash
½ teaspoon salt
2 tablespoons vinegar
2 tablespoons butter
1 teaspoon paprika
1 tablespoon finely chopped dill
2 tablespoons flour
½ cup heavy sweet or sour cream

4 TO 6 SERVINGS

Cut the squash into narrow strips and sprinkle lightly with the salt and vinegar. Let stand 15 minutes, then drain off the moisture. Place in a covered pan with the butter and simmer until tender but not soft. Stir in the paprika, dill, and flour. Add the cream and stir until mixture is smooth and thickened. The flavor is enhanced if liquid from fermented cucumbers is used in the sauce, before the cream is added.

Variation: Use 1 cup of strained canned tomatoes instead of cream to make the sauce.

POTATOES SOUR STYLE

SAVANYÚ BURGONYAFŐZELÉK

6 SERVINGS

6 medium-size potatoes, pared
1 teaspoon salt
1 bay leaf
1½ cups boiling water
2 tablespoons fat
2 tablespoons flour
⅛ teaspoon black pepper
2 tablespoons vinegar
½ cup sour cream

Cook the potatoes with the salt and bay leaf in the boiling water until tender. Reserve the cooking water. Remove the bay leaves and cube the potatoes. Blend the fat and flour over low heat. Add the water from the cooked potatoes, the pepper, and the vinegar. Stir over heat until thickened. Combine with the potatoes add the cream, and cover for 5 minutes before serving.

RICE WITH PEAS

RIZIBIZI

6 SERVINGS

1 pound fresh peas in pods
2 cups boiling water
1 teaspoon salt
2 tablespoons butter
1 tablespoon chopped parsley
1 onion, chopped
¼ cup rice

Wash and shell the peas. Cook the pods in the water with the salt. Discard the pods and cook rice until tender in the water. Combine the butter, parsley, and onion and heat to brown slightly. Add the peas, then slowly add the rice. Cook together 5 minutes before serving.

LAYER SAUERKRAUT

RAKOTT KÁPOSZTA

8 SERVINGS

3 cups sauerkraut
1 pound smoked pork or ham
¼ cup rice
4 slices bacon
4 link sausages
2 teaspoons paprika
2 hard-cooked eggs
1 cup sour cream

Rinse the sauerkraut with clear water. Add fresh water to cover and cook with the pork until both are well done. Drain liquid into a large kettle, bring to a rolling boil, add the rice, and boil until it is tender. Cut the pork into small pieces. Fry the bacon and sausage. Remove from fat, and brown the pork in the fat. Stir in the paprika. Drain the rice. Arrange layers in a baking dish, starting with bacon, then sauerkraut, pork, rice, and cream. Slice the eggs and the sausages over these, and add more rice and sauerkraut, then top with cream. Heat in a moderate oven (350° F.) for 25 minutes.

LAYER SAVOY CABBAGE

RAKOTT KELKÁPOSZTA

8 SERVINGS

2 savoy cabbages
1 teaspoon salt
4 tablespoons butter
1 cup sour cream
½ cup bread crumbs

Cook cabbage in boiling salted water for 10 minutes. Drain. Separate leaves. Butter a baking dish and arrange in it layers of cabbage leaves. Dot each layer with pieces of butter and 2 or 3 spoonfuls of sour cream. Repeat until cabbage is used. Top with bread crumbs which have been browned in butter. Bake in oven for 15 minutes.

SORREL WITH CREAM

SÓSKAFŐZELÉK

1 pound sorrel
1 small onion, chopped
2 tablespoons fat
2 tablespoons flour
1 teaspoon salt
1/8 teaspoon pepper
1/2 cup stock
1/2 cup sour cream

6 SERVINGS

Heat the sorrel in slightly salted water until wilted, about 5 minutes. Drain and chop. Brown the onion in the fat, add the flour, salt, and pepper. Stir. Thin with the stock and stir until mixture boils. Combine with the sorrel. A few minutes before serving, stir in the cream.

SPINACH PUDDING

SPENÓTPUDDING

1/4 cup butter
1/2 teaspoon salt
1/4 cup potato flour
1/2 cup medium cream
4 eggs, separated
1 cup cooked spinach
1/4 cup chopped cooked ham

6 SERVINGS

In the top of a large double boiler, blend the butter, salt, and potato flour over hot water. Add the cream and the egg yolks, and stir until thick and smooth. Remove from the heat and cover to prevent drying on top. Grind the spinach, or finely chop it. Combine with the ham and blend into the sauce. Beat the egg whites stiff and fold into the spinach mixture. Cover and return to the heat; steam for an hour without lifting the lid. Serve at once.

SALADS, RELISHES, AND SAUCES

SALADS, RELISHES, AND SAUCES

Salads of the American type are not generally served or eaten in Hungary, though there is an increasing interest in foreign dishes. The salads that are typically Hungarian and popular the year round are potato salad, cabbage salad, and knob celery salad. In season, side dishes of fresh cucumbers with sour cream, tomatoes, cantaloupe, and chestnuts with vegetables vary the menu. Relishes such as beets in vinegar, pickled green and red peppers, pickled cucumbers, and fermented dill pickles take the place of our salads and are considered accents to more basic dishes.

Mixed greens or combinations of vegetables, or fruits served with mayonnaise or a thin dressing, are considered French or English dishes. Although they are undoubtedly used at lavish buffet suppers, they rarely appear on the average family table, though lettuce is frequently seen when available.

Hungarian sauces are served with the meat or main dish. They are rich or tart, always well seasoned, and usually have heavy sweet or sour cream added just before being brought to the table. They serve much the same purpose as relishes in that they provide contrast in texture and flavor.

CANTALOUPE IN SOUR CREAM

TEJFÖLÖS SÁRGADINNYE

6 SERVINGS

1 ripe cantaloupe, chilled
Salt
Pepper
¼ cup mayonnaise
3 tablespoons sour cream

Cut the cantaloupe into halves, remove seeds, and divide into 1-inch sections. Cut from the rind and cube. Sprinkle with salt and pepper. Combine mayonnaise and cream. Add to the cantaloupe and stir with a fork. Chill and serve on lettuce.

ORANGE SALAD

NARANCSSALÁTA

6 SERVINGS

6 oranges
2 tablespoons powdered sugar
4 tablespoons orange liqueur
2 tablespoons red wine

Skin oranges, remove pulp and seeds. Cut in thin slices and arrange on glass platter. Sprinkle with powdered sugar. Add orange liqueur and wine. Chill thoroughly before serving.

CHESTNUTS WITH VEGETABLES

GESZTENYESALÁTA

1 pound chestnuts
1 knob celery
1 teaspoon salt
¼ cup wine vinegar
⅓ cup salad oil

1 teaspoon dry mustard
½ teaspoon salt
⅛ teaspoon pepper
1 small, firm head lettuce, sliced
3 cooked beets, sliced
3 hard-cooked eggs, sliced

8 SERVINGS

Remove the outer shells from the chestnuts. Boil them with the knob celery and the 1 teaspoon salt, in enough water to cover, until tender. Put the vinegar, oil, mustard, ½ teaspoon salt, and pepper in a jar with a tight cover and shake well. Peel the brown coating from the hot chestnuts and break into halves. Peel and slice the knob celery. Combine the chestnuts and celery with the dressing, add the lettuce, beets, and eggs, and chill.

CUCUMBERS WITH SOUR CREAM

TEJFÖLÖS UBORKA

4 large cucumbers
2 teaspoons salt
¼ cup wine vinegar
½ teaspoon paprika
2 tablespoons salad oil
¼ cup heavy sweet or sour cream

6 SERVINGS

Peel the cucumbers and slice thin. Sprinkle with the salt and let stand 15 minutes. Drain and press out the moisture. Add the vinegar and paprika. A few minutes before serving add the salad oil and cream.

Note: ⅛ teaspoon black pepper may be substituted for the paprika.

KNOB CELERY AND TOMATO SALAD

ZELLER-ÉS PARADICSOMSALÁTA

6 SERVINGS

3 knob celery roots
½ cup water
Juice of ½ lemon
2 tablespoons salad oil
½ teaspoon salt
⅛ teaspoon pepper
¼ cup mayonnaise
6 lettuce leaves
3 tomatoes, sliced
1 green pepper, sliced

Peel the knob celery and slice thin. Boil the water, add the lemon juice, oil, salt, pepper, and celery slices. Cover tightly and cook over low heat until nearly tender. Increase heat to boil away any water remaining. Cool and mix with mayonnaise. Serve on lettuce garnished with tomato and green pepper slices.

EGGPLANT SALAD

TÖRÖK PADLIZSÁN-SALÁTA

6 SERVINGS

1 eggplant
1 small onion, grated
1 teaspoon sugar
2 tablespoons lemon juice
½ teaspoon salt
1 tablespoon salad oil
2 tomatoes, sliced
Parsley

Pierce holes in the eggplant with a fork. Place in a glass baking dish and bake in a hot oven (400° F.) until tender. Cool slightly and peel. Chop fine. Combine the onion, sugar, lemon juice, and salt and stir into the eggplant. Cool. Just before serving add the salad oil. Heap in the center of a platter and garnish with tomato slices and parsley.

KNOB CELERY AND POTATO SALAD

ZELLER-ÉS BURGONYASALÁTA

3 medium-size potatoes
3 small knob celery roots
3 pickled beets
1 hard-cooked egg
Lettuce
Parsley
4 tablespoons lemon juice
4 tablespoons salad oil
1 teaspoon paprika

6 SERVINGS

Cook the potatoes and knob celery in salted water until tender. Peel and slice thin. Chill. Slice the beets and egg. Arrange on lettuce alternate slices of potato, celery, beet, and egg. Garnish with parsley. Combine the lemon juice, oil, and paprika. Shake well and pour over the salad.

KOHLRABI SALAD

KALARÁBÉSALÁTA

3 young kohlrabi
2 tablespoons butter
¼ cup french dressing or Mayonnaise

6 SERVINGS

Peel the kohlrabi and slice thin. Heat the butter in a tightly covered pan. Add the kohlrabi, cover, and cook slowly until tender, about 15 minutes. Chill and serve mixed with the dressing.

LETTUCE WITH SOUR CREAM AND CRACKLINGS

ÖNTÖTT SALÁTA

1 head lettuce
4 strips bacon
½ cup vinegar
½ cup water
1 teaspoon salt
⅛ teaspoon pepper or paprika
½ cup sour cream

6 SERVINGS

Cut the lettuce into 6 sections. Cut the bacon into squares, fry until crisp, and remove to absorbent paper. Pour off the bacon fat, retaining about 1 tablespoon in the skillet. Add the vinegar, water, salt, and pepper, and bring to a boil. Pour over the lettuce and drain off immediately. Arrange the lettuce on a platter or on individual plates; top with the sour cream and garnish with the bacon cracklings.

PICKLED BEETS

CÉKLA

6 medium-size beets
½ teaspoon caraway seeds
1 teaspoon salt
1 tablespoon horseradish
3 tablespoons sugar
½ cup vinegar
¼ cup water

6 SERVINGS

Boil beets until tender; peel and slice. In a wide-mouthed jar arrange layers of beet slices, caraway seeds, salt, and horseradish. Combine the sugar, vinegar, and water and cover the beets with it. Let stand in the refrigerator several hours before serving. They will be equally good after several days.

HERRING SALAD

HERINGSALÁTA

2 pickled herrings
3 hard-cooked eggs
2 medium-size boiled potatoes
2 raw apples
1 tablespoon chopped onion
¼ cup vinegar
¼ cup salad oil
½ teaspoon prepared mustard
½ teaspoon salt
¼ teaspoon pepper

6 SERVINGS

Slice the herring into small pieces. Dice the eggs, potatoes, and apples. Add the onion. Blend the vinegar, oil, mustard, salt, and pepper together. Combine all the ingredients and let stand 30 minutes before serving.

BÉCHAMEL SAUCE

BESAMEL MÁRTÁS

4 tablespoons flour
4 tablespoons butter
1 teaspoon salt
2½ cups cream or milk
2 egg yolks, slightly beaten

ABOUT 3 CUPS

Mix the flour, butter, and salt over boiling water. Gradually stir in the liquid and cook until smooth and thickened. Stir a few tablespoons of the sauce into the egg yolks, then combine. This is excellent on vegetables, hot or cold, or with boiled fish.

CUCUMBER SAUCE

UBORKAMÁRTÁS

2 tablespoons butter
2 tablespoons flour

¼ teaspoon salt
⅔ cup meat stock
3 medium-size pickled cucumbers, finely chopped
½ cup heavy cream

ABOUT 1¼ CUPS

Blend the butter, flour, and salt over boiling water. Stir in the meat stock and cook until smooth and thickened. Add the cucumbers and cream and mix well. Serve with boiled fish.

CURRANT SAUCE

RIBIZKEMÁRTÁS

½ cup currant jam
2 tablespoons butter
2 tablespoons flour
½ cup meat stock
1 tablespoon lemon juice
½ cup heavy cream

ABOUT 1½ CUPS

Combine butter and flour and stir over boiling water. Add meat stock and cook until smooth. Add currant jam and lemon juice and mix well. Before serving, blend with cream.

DILL SAUCE

KAPORMÁRTÁS

2 tablespoons butter
2 tablespoons flour
½ teaspoon salt
½ cup meat stock
1 tablespoon chopped dill
½ cup sour cream

ABOUT 1 CUP

Blend the butter, flour, and salt over boiling water. Stir in the meat stock and cook until smooth and thickened. Add the dill and the sour cream and mix. Serve with boiled soup meat.

HORSERADISH SAUCE

TORMAMÁRTÁS

3 tablespoons flour
¼ teaspoon salt
1 cup heavy cream
4 tablespoons grated horseradish
½ cup soup stock

ABOUT 1½ CUPS

Blend the flour and salt with half the cream. When smooth, add the rest of the cream. Combine and heat the horseradish and soup stock. Stir in the cream mixture and cook until smooth and thickened.

MUSHROOM SAUCE

GOMBAMÁRTÁS

1 onion, finely chopped
1 pound mushrooms, sliced
2 tablespoons butter
2 tablespoons finely chopped parsley
2 tablespoons flour
1 tablespoon lemon juice
¾ cup heavy cream

ABOUT 2 CUPS

Brown the onion and the mushrooms in the butter. Stir in the parsley and the flour. Add the lemon juice, then the cream. Cook until thickened, stirring constantly.

WINE SAUCE

BORMÁRTÁS

2 egg yolks
2 tablespoons sugar
½ cup white wine
1 tablespoon lemon juice

ABOUT 1 CUP

Beat the egg yolks and sugar until thick and lemon-colored.

Transfer to double boiler, add the wine and lemon juice, and continue beating over boiling water until thickened.

GOOSEBERRY SAUCE

EGRESMÁRTÁS

2 cups gooseberries
2 tablespoons butter
2 tablespoons flour
2 egg yolks
¼ teaspoon salt
½ cup sugar
¼ cup (or more) meat stock
½ cup sour cream

ABOUT 1 CUP

Cook the gooseberries in the butter. Blend the flour, egg yolks, salt, and sugar with the meat stock. Stir into the gooseberries and cook until thickened. Before serving, add the sour cream. Serve with chicken or turkey.

BREADS AND NOODLES

The picturesque ceremony of blessing the wheat fields on St. Mark's Day, April twenty-fifth, is traditional in Hungary. It is a solemn event observed in Hungarian churches, even in this country. In old Hungary the priest and his parishioners would go to the wheat fields and chant this invocation of the Lord's grace: ". . . so that fog shall not strangle, hail shall not batter, storm shall not break, and fire shall not destroy the only hope of a poor nation." Elsewhere villagers take freshly made bread to church where, in prayer, they invoke the blessing of the Lord on the wheat yield.

These rites symbolize the people's appreciation of the all-important wheat grain, the crop upon which this agricultural country still depends. Bread, rolls, and the various kinds of noodles and dumplings are the mainstays of the Hungarian laboring people. So necessary is wheat to the livelihood and the dinner table of a large part of the population that a failure in the crop could mean much hunger.

Little wonder that the completed harvest is marked by elation and feasting. Late in June—usually the twenty-ninth, St. Peter's and St. Paul's Day—the wheat harvest begins. It is a critical day. Harvest must be completed in the shortest possible time, because the ripe heads easily spill the heavy grain, and rain would ruin the crop. Mechanical reapers are not common in Hungary, so all hands "turn to" and help with the cutting and binding—still largely hand processes, shared by men and women, boys and girls.

A jubilant harvest festival follows the cutting of the wheat; another comes after the corn husking and the wine harvest in early autumn. Though corn, corn meal, and rye are much used, wheat is far more important. The rich glutenous flour made from the hard, Hungarian winter wheat is unexcelled for noodle products, pastries, strudels, and breads. This high-quality flour is also in demand all over Europe for use in fine pastries and strudels.

Hungarian families have their own varieties of flour "mixings" for bread and rolls. Villages develop typical blends, using the various grains produced locally. Commercial flour is more uniform, but it, too, is unbleached and produces a creamy white loaf. Fragrant black bread is popular, as are dark rye and light rye with caraway seeds.

Nothing is more tempting to rich or poor than homemade bread. There is recurrent excitement over the results of the weekly baking, and great joy when the loaves are perfect. The simpler the household, the more important this event.

Boiled pastry becomes a substantial part of many Hungarian meals. It may be the main dish, or an accompaniment to it, or one of the most favored desserts. All Hungarian boiled pastry contains egg, and it may have varying amounts of water to moisten the flour. *Gombóc* (dumplings) and *galuska* (soft noodles) are moist, while *metélt* (noodles) and *csipetke* (pinched noodles) are nearly dry. *Tarhonya* (egg barley) becomes completely dry before cooking. Recipes for these interesting Hungarian dishes follow.

BISCUITS WITH CRACKLINGS

TÖPÖRTYŰS POGÁCSA

½ package granular yeast
2 tablespoons lukewarm water
1 teaspoon sugar
1 teaspoon salt
1 teaspoon pepper
2 eggs
1 cup cracklings or crisp chopped bacon
½ cup sour cream
2 cups sifted flour
1 egg yolk

15 TO 20 BISCUITS

Soak the yeast in the lukewarm water with the sugar added. After 10 minutes blend in the salt, pepper, whole eggs, cracklings, and cream. Stir in the flour and knead well. Roll out ½ inch thick. Cut into 2-inch rounds and arrange on an ungreased baking sheet. Make diagonal cuts in the top of each biscuit, brush with egg yolk, and let rise in a warm place for 30 minutes. Bake in a moderate oven (350° F.) until browned, about 15 minutes.

COTTAGE CHEESE BISCUITS

TÚRÓS POGÁCSA

1 cup sifted flour
½ teaspoon salt
½ cup cold butter
½ cup cottage cheese
1 egg yolk
1 tablespoon caraway seeds

ABOUT 12 BISCUITS

Sift together the flour and salt, then quickly chop in the butter and cheese. (The butter should remain hard.) Press the dough together to form a ball; flatten and fold over 4 times. Chill until firm. Roll out ⅛ inch thick, fold over 4 times, and chill again. Repeat the folding and chilling process 3 times. Roll out ¼ inch thick; cut into 2-inch rounds, mark with lattice lines, brush with egg yolk, and sprinkle with caraway seeds. Bake in a hot oven (400° F.) for about 10 minutes, or until golden.

YEAST DOUGH RAISED IN WATER

VIZBEN KELT TÉSZTA

1 package granular yeast
¼ cup lukewarm water
2 tablespoons sugar
1 teaspoon salt
2 tablespoons softened butter
6 egg yolks
¾ cup lukewarm milk
4 cups flour
½ cup chopped nuts
½ cup brown sugar
Grated rind of 1 lemon

30 TO 40 ROLLS

Soak the yeast in the lukewarm water for 15 minutes. When the yeast is dissolved, stir in the sugar, salt, butter, egg yolks, milk, and half the flour. Beat vigorously until mixture is well blended and smooth. Stir in the rest of the flour and mix until blisters appear and dough is elastic.

Thoroughly grease a large table napkin; turn dough into it, and lap edges so there are no openings. Gather up loosely, allowing space for dough to rise to double the size, and tie with a string. Place in a large kettle of cold water and let dough rise until double in bulk (about 6 hours). Meantime mix the nuts, brown sugar, and lemon rind.

Turn dough onto a well-floured board and knead into a firm ball. Cut into small dumplings, about 2 inches across. Roll each in the nut mixture. Place dumplings so they touch each other in a greased baking pan. Let rise in a warm place (free from drafts) until double in size. Bake in a moderately hot oven (375° F.) until golden brown, about 35 minutes.

POTATO BISCUITS

BURGONYÁPOGÁCSA

1 teaspoon salt
1¾ cups sifted flour
1 cup cold butter
2 tablespoons sour cream
1 cup cold mashed potatoes
4 egg yolks
2 tablespoons caraway seeds

ABOUT 24 BISCUITS

Sift the salt with the flour. Cut in the butter until well mixed. Add the cream, potatoes, and 3 of the egg yolks. Stir and knead together. Roll thin. Fold over 4 times and chill until firm. Repeat the rolling, folding, and chilling process 3 times. Roll out ¼ inch thick, brush with remaining egg yolk, and sprinkle with caraway seeds. Bake in a hot oven (400° F.) about 15 minutes, or until light brown.

NOODLES

METÉLTEK

1⅓ cups sifted flour
½ teaspoon salt
1 egg
2 tablespoons water

6 SERVINGS

This noodle pastry is suitable for soup, main dish, or dessert.

Mix together the flour and salt. Break the egg into the center of the flour, add the water, and mix all together. Knead thoroughly until the dough is smooth and velvety. Put flour on your hands and shape dough into a loaf. Cover and let stand 15 minutes, to make rolling easier.

On a floured board, roll out the dough tissue-thin. Divide in half if it becomes too large for the board. Slightly dry the sheets of dough on a cloth. Roll each into a tight scroll and slice thin. Scatter the noodles as they are cut, to dry them further.

Note: Instead of rolling up for cutting, the thin pastry may be stacked in strips and cut into 1-inch squares; or it may be rolled less thin and torn into csipetke (*pinched noodles*).

NOODLES WITH CHOPPED MEAT

RAKOTT METÉLT VAGDALTHÚSSAL

6 SERVINGS

½ pound ground veal, beef, or pork
1 tablespoon butter
1 tablespoon chopped parsley
1 pound (about 3 cups) fine noodles
8 cups boiling salted water
1 tablespoon bacon fat or butter
½ cup grated cheese
¼ cup sour cream

Brown the meat in the butter; add the parsley. Slowly turn the noodles into boiling water and boil until tender, about 12 minutes. Drain, rinse with hot water, and stir into the hot bacon fat or butter. Then in a greased baking dish arrange alternate layers of noodles, meat, and cheese. Top with the cream and bake in a slow oven (325° F.) for 30 minutes.

CABBAGE WITH NOODLE SQUARES

KÁPOSZTÁSKOCZKA

3 cups finely chopped cabbage
1 teaspoon salt
2 tablespoons fat
1 tablespoon sugar
Noodles, cut in squares
1 teaspoon pepper

6 SERVINGS

Mix the cabbage with the salt and let stand 30 minutes. Press the cabbage to squeeze out moisture. Brown in the fat, which has been heated with the sugar. Add pepper. Cover after 5 minutes and cook until done. Cook the noodles in boiling salted water until tender, about 12 minutes. Drain and rinse with hot water. Combine with the cooked cabbage, heat, and serve.

EGG BARLEY

TARHONYA

4 cups sifted flour
1 teaspoon salt
3 large eggs

12 SERVINGS

Mix all ingredients into a hard dough and knead thoroughly. Roll and cut into ⅛-inch strips; then chop off small pieces. Continue chopping until the pieces are as fine as barley grains. Spread out on large baking sheets and dry out in a slightly warm oven. Store in jars, to be cooked later in soups or used as an accompaniment to meats.

TOASTED EGG BARLEY

PIRITOTT TARHONYA

6 SERVINGS

1 cup Egg Barley
2 tablespoons bacon fat
½ teaspoon salt
1 teaspoon paprika (optional)

Lightly brown the dry egg barley in the fat, add the salt and paprika, and cover with water. Simmer until the water is absorbed, about 15 minutes. Cover, and finish cooking in a moderate oven (350° F.) until tender, an hour or more, depending on the size of the pieces. It should remain flaky like well-cooked rice.

POTATO DUMPLINGS

BURGONYAGOMBÓC

6 SERVINGS

2 cups potatoes, cooked and peeled
1 tablespoon butter
½ teaspoon salt
3 eggs
1 cup ¼-inch bread cubes, dried
3 tablespoons fat

Press the potatoes through a strainer. Combine the butter, salt, and eggs, then mix with the potatoes. Lightly brown the bread cubes in the fat, and stir into the potato mixture. Shape into small dumplings and cook in gently boiling salted water about 15 minutes. Avoid overcooking or the dumplings may break apart. Serve immediately.

Note: If made very small, these dumplings are good in meat or chicken soup. Larger dumplings may be rolled in buttered crumbs, then in confectioners' sugar, and served as dessert.

SOFT NOODLES

GALUSKA

6 SERVINGS

2 cups sifted flour
¾ cup water
1 egg
1 teaspoon salt

Mix all ingredients lightly until well blended. Put a portion of the dough on a small wet breadboard, and cut with a wet knife into 1-inch-wide strips. From these strips cut 1-inch pieces and push them off into boiling salted water. They are done when they rise to the top. Skim them off and pile in a hot dish. Serve with Paprika Chicken or Goulash.

PINCHED OR TORN NOODLES

CSIPETKE

6 SERVINGS

1 cup sifted flour
½ teaspoon salt
2 eggs

Mix together the flour and salt. Break the eggs into the center of the flour and stir to make a stiff dough. Knead until smooth and velvety. Roll out to ¼-inch thickness. Pinch off bits of the dough as large as hazelnuts, and drop into boiling salted water or into boiling soup. Cook about 15 minutes, or until tender.

PANCAKES

Pancakes, or *palacsinták* as they are known in Hungary, have a long history but boast no one national origin. Egyptians cooked them on flat stones in the hot sun, and they were a favored food of early Roman armies. During the Middle Ages the Roman Catholic Church designated Shrove Tuesday as a day for the eating of pancakes because of their symbolic ingredients. Flour represented the staff of life, milk stood for innocence, salt for wholesomeness, and eggs, the basic Lenten food, symbolized fertility.

Today pancakes are universally popular. Their variety ranges from the rough-and-ready flapjack or griddlecake, the typically American breakfast favorite, to the fancy French dessert or crêpe Suzette served with flaming sauce.

Keeping *palacsinták* an exciting treat is the pride of the Hungarian housewife. She serves them for dinner at noon or for supper—never for breakfast. They are extra special as an entree and are enthusiastically welcomed for the main dish or as a dessert of rare excellence.

Only the finest of fresh ingredients go into a *palacsinta tészta* (pancake batter), though proportions vary according to use.

There may be few or many eggs, much or little milk—and this often mixed with water—a little unsalted butter or none at all, and sugar if sweetness is desired. The batter is quickly and easily mixed; a little stirring makes it creamy smooth. Sometimes egg whites are beaten and added with the last, more gentle stirring. The batter will be no thicker than sweet heavy cream, and the baked *palacsinta*, with few exceptions, will be wafer-thin. It should always be tender, fragrantly tempting, and of superlatively good flavor.

The *palacsinta* is not browned like its distant cousin, the thicker American griddlecake, but remains transparent and golden. The moment it is baked, Hungarian originality begins, and there seems to be no limit to the wondrous ways these delicately thin and tender cakes may be served. They are rolled, folded, or layered twelve to fifteen high for slicing pie-fashion—always with a favorite spread. Hungarians are partial to ham-filled *palacsinta* as an entree. Cabbage, spinach, and mushroom *palacsinta* make inexpensive main dishes which are well liked. Most delectable of all are those prepared for dessert. These are spread with apricot, strawberry, or raspberry jam, with almond or walnut filling, or with cottage cheese.

Palacsinták are also served singly, fresh from the griddle and topped with sugar, jam, or finely ground nuts in sour cream. Then there is the Hungarian specialty of paprika-chicken pancake noodles with sour cream. Such tantalizing goodness is in and between those thin delicate pancakes, however arranged, that it's small wonder they are so eagerly received. Hearty appetites are teased back for more and more and still one more *palacsinta*.

POINTERS FOR HUNGARIAN PALACSINTA

1

Bake pancakes one at a time, as native Hungarians do, on a bevel-edged skillet. When a few drops of water will dance on it, the skillet is hot enough for even browning. Grease it with unsalted butter before baking each pancake. Butter is best for flavor but Hungarians also use fine lard.

2

For an 8-inch pancake, dip ¼ cup of batter onto the hot greased skillet. With a quick rotary motion tip the skillet to spread the batter thinly. The baked *palacsinta* should be transparently thin. A batter with beaten egg whites should be stirred before each dipping as the whites tend to rise and separate. A fluffy batter will bake a thicker *palacsinta* but once off the griddle it, too, will become thin.

3

Brown the *palacsinta* only very lightly. During the first browning it will become firm enough to be easily turned. When the second side is tinged brown, ease the cake onto a warm platter or baking dish. Spread filling on the baked *palacsinta* while another is cooking. Even spreading is not essential as the warmth of the pancake distributes the filling. Roll or fold each *palacsinta* or arrange a number of them in layers.

4

When all are baked, reheat in a moderate oven (350° F) for about 20 minutes; serve hot. An extra *palacsinta* placed over a dish of rolled ones will keep them moist in the oven. Remove this top one before serving.

PLAIN PANCAKES

PALACSINTATÉSZTA

20 TO 24 PANCAKES

2 cups sifted flour
1 teaspoon salt
4 eggs, separated
3 cups milk or equal parts milk and water

Combine flour, salt, egg yolks, and 1 cup of the milk, stirring until smooth. Gradually stir in the rest of the milk to make a batter the consistency of heavy sweet cream. Beat egg whites until stiff but not dry and fold into the batter. Stir again before dipping each pancake. Bake full-size thin cakes on an 8-inch skillet, tipping to spread batter.

Combine with meat, fish, or vegetable filling for main dish of entree. This batter may also be used for dessert pancakes served with sweet fillings or toppings.

Variation: Use 2 instead of 4 eggs and add them, unbeaten, with the first cup of milk. The thin cakes from this batter will be less delicate to handle than those with more eggs, and make a thriftier main dish.

LAYER HAM PANCAKES

RAKOTT SONKÁSPALACSINTA

Prepare Plain Pancakes and arrange in layers with the following filling:

HAM FILLING

8 TO 10 SERVINGS

1 pound chopped boiled ham
2 egg yolks
1 cup sour cream

Combine the ham, egg yolks, and cream. Place a freshly baked pancake on a buttered baking dish; spread with 1 tablespoon of filling and repeat until you have many layers. Only the top cake should be buttered. Place in moderate oven (350° F.) until filling is set, usually about 20 minutes. Cut pie-fashion and serve hot.

FRIED HAM PANCAKES

KIRÁNTOTT SONKÁSPALACSINTA

This is a crispy entree. Bake Plain Pancakes extra thin for rolling. Spread 1 tablespoon Ham Filling (see preceding recipe) on each. Roll up and tuck in ends. Lightly beat 2 egg whites or 1 whole egg. Dip rolled cakes first in egg, then in flour, again in egg, and finally in bread crumbs. Fry in deep fat until crust is light brown. Serve at once.

ABOUT 24 ROLLS

LOBSTER-FILLED PANCAKES

RÁKKAL TÖLTÖTT PALACSINTA

8 TO 10 SERVINGS

Plain Pancakes
½ cup mushrooms, finely chopped
1 tablespoon butter
1 cup cooked lobster or crab meat
1 tablespoon chopped parsley
½ teaspoon salt
Dash of pepper
½ cup sour cream
1 baker's roll or
1 slice white bread softened in milk

Brown mushrooms lightly in butter and allow to cool. Combine all ingredients. Using this filling, follow procedure as for Layer Ham Pancakes.

MUSHROOM-FILLED PANCAKES

GOMBÁVAL TÖLTÖTT PALACSINTA

Plain Pancakes
1½ cups finely chopped mushrooms
2 tablespoons butter
½ teaspoon salt
Dash of pepper
½ cup sour cream
1 egg, slightly beaten

8 TO 10 SERVINGS

Brown mushrooms in butter; cool slightly, then combine with the salt and pepper, sour cream, and egg. Using this filling, proceed as for Layer Ham Pancakes.

PAPRIKA-CHICKEN PANCAKE NOODLES

PAPRIKÁSCSIRKÉS PALACSINTA

This dish is good heated and served in an earthenware casserole or skillet. It is a favorite with native Hungarians.

Plain Pancakes
2 cups chopped Paprika Chicken
1 cup sour cream

6 TO 8 SERVINGS

Cut the baked pancakes into ½-inch strips (or pancake noodles). Mix the chicken with sour cream; combine with the noodles.

Turn into a greased casserole and bake in a moderate oven (350° F.) 20 to 30 minutes. Serve from casserole.

Note: Borjúpaprikás (*Veal Paprika*) *may replace chicken in this recipe.*

CABBAGE PANCAKES

KÁPOSZTÁSPALACSINTA

For a vegetable main dish, use this filling.

6 TO 8 SERVINGS

Plain Pancakes
2 cups finely chopped cabbage
½ teaspoon salt
Dash of pepper
2 tablespoons butter

Mix the cabbage with salt and pepper. Brown in butter until tender. Cool, then fold into the pancake batter. Make somewhat thicker cakes than usual. Serve hot from the griddle.

Note: Chopped ham or cooked spinach may be used instead of cabbage.

PANCAKE DOUGHNUTS

PALACSINTAFÁNK

8 SERVINGS

Plain Pancakes—Variation
½ cup ground cooked ham or beef
½ cup ground cooked mushrooms
2 eggs, separated
2 tablespoons sour cream
Hot fat

Mix together the meat, mushrooms, egg yolks, and cream. With a cooky cutter, make small rounds from the pancakes. Spread half of them with the filling. Brush the edges with egg white and top with the other rounds. Press the edges together. Brown the filled rounds in hot fat for a few minutes. Serve them hot with green vegetables.

Note: The remnants of the pancakes may be cut in strips, topped with ground sugared walnuts, and eaten as dessert.

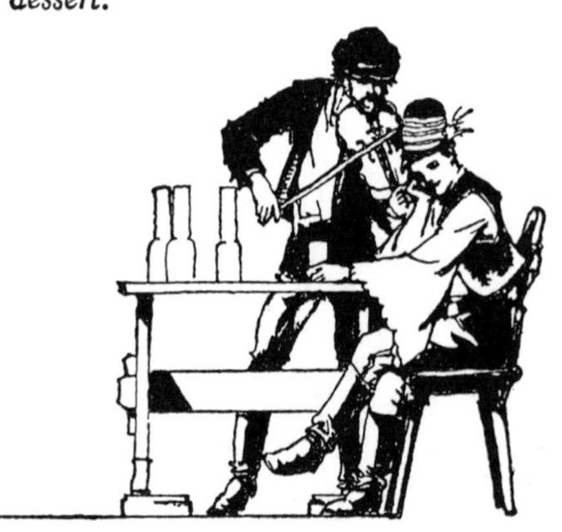

PANCAKE SOUFFLÉ

PALACSINTAFELFUJT

6 SERVINGS

Plain Pancakes—Variation
1 cup ground cooked ham or smoked pork tenderloin
4 eggs, separated
1 cup sour cream

Cut the baked pancakes into ½-inch strips. Mix the meat, egg yolks, and sour cream. Beat the egg whites until they stand in peaks. Fold the egg mixtures together, then fold in the pancake strips. Butter the inside of the top part of a double boiler. Pour the mixture into it; cover, set over hot water, and steam for 1 hour. Turn out on a platter and serve at once.

DESSERT PANCAKES

ÉDES
PALACSINTATÉSZTA

These pancakes are excellent with cottage cheese, a nut filling, or with a favorite jam.

2 cups sifted flour
½ teaspoon salt
1 tablespoon sugar
3 cups milk
4 eggs, separated

15 TO 20 PANCAKES

Combine flour, salt, sugar, 1 cup of the milk, and the egg yolks, stirring until smooth. Gradually stir in the rest of the milk to make a creamy batter. Beat the egg whites until stiff but not dry and fold into the batter. Stir again before dipping out each pancake. Bake paper-thin for rolling. Tip the skillet with a rotary motion to spread the batter evenly. Brown pancakes lightly on each side. Spread with one of the fillings below, and roll.

CHOCOLATE PANCAKE DESSERT

CSOKOLÁDÉS PALACSINTA

¼ cup butter
¼ cup sugar
⅔ cup flour
2 cups milk
½ teaspoon vanilla
8 eggs, separated
2 ounces (¼ bar) semi-sweet chocolate

8 SERVINGS

In the top of a double boiler, melt the butter; stir in the sugar and flour. Gradually blend in the milk, stirring constantly, until mixture becomes very thick and smooth. Remove from heat, cool slightly, add the vanilla, and blend in the egg yolks. Beat the egg whites till they stand in peaks; then fold the batter into them.

Bake 6-inch, fluffy pancakes. They will be tender and require careful handling. When lightly browned on both sides, place the first cake in a baking dish. Sprinkle with grated sweet chocolate and keep in a warm oven. Top with the next cake. Continue until there are 3 or 4 layers. Proceed until all are baked. Then garnish with Meringue Topping, given below.

MERINGUE TOPPING

3 egg whites
½ teaspoon vanilla
3 tablespoons sugar

Beat the egg whites until they stand in peaks; fold in the vanilla and sugar. Pile the mixture on the stacked pancakes and brown lightly in a slow oven (325° F.). Serve warm, cut pie-fashion.

RICH DESSERT PANCAKES

CSUSZTATOTT
PALACSINTA

This is a rich pancake, delicate and sweet. It requires no filling.

¼ cup butter
¼ cup sugar
¼ teaspoon salt
5 eggs, separated
¼ cup sifted flour
½ cup milk
¼ teaspoon vanilla
Sugar

6 SERVINGS

Cream together the butter, sugar, and salt; add the egg yolks and beat well. Stir in the flour and then the milk. Beat the egg whites until stiff but not dry, add the vanilla, and fold into the batter. With unsalted butter, grease a hot skillet or griddle, and pour less than ¼ cup of batter onto it. Do not tip or spread. These pancakes will be 5 or 6 inches across and about ¼ inch thick while baking.

Brown lightly on one side only, then slip onto a baking dish and set in a slow oven (300° F.). Sprinkle a little sugar on the uncooked surface of each pancake before placing the next one on top of it. Continue until there are 5 layers, then start another stack. Let them remain in a slow oven 15 or 20 minutes longer, or until the top is delicately brown. Serve at once, cut pie-fashion.

COTTAGE CHEESE FILLING

TÚRÓS TÖLTELÉK

This filling is a favorite in Hungary. It is amazingly simple to make and just as amazingly good to eat.

2 cups cottage cheese
1 egg yolk
2 tablespoons sugar
½ cup sour cream
½ cup raisins

Press the cottage cheese through a sieve or mash with a fork until well creamed. Mix with the egg yolk, sugar, cream, and raisins. Spread each pancake with 1 tablespoon of the cheese mixture, roll up, arrange in a baking dish, and reheat in a moderate oven (350° F.) for 20 minutes.

Note: Many prefer dessert pancakes with apricot, strawberry, or raspberry jam. A richer filling results from a mix-

ture of ½ cup crushed, blanched almonds, 1 egg yolk, 2 tablespoons sugar, and ¼ cup sour cream.

STRUDELS AND PASTRIES

STRUDELS AND PASTRIES

Of all Hungarian foods, strudels and the *Dobos torta* (many-layered cake) are probably the most distinctive. They are a challenge—and a compliment—to any cook when they turn out well, for they are made of about nine tenths skill and one tenth fine ingredients.

The origin of the strudel is controversial but one fact is accepted. Hungarian cooks have developed the art of making it to high perfection from the rich, glutenous flour, produced in Hungary and so carefully milled that is the finest obtainable for strudel making.

Successful bakers of strudels handle the dough differently, adding more or less moisture, stretching the dough a little thinner or letting it dry a bit longer than the directions suggest but they use one basic recipe. Fillings, of course, may be as varied as the imagination. Apple, cheese, cherry, and cabbage fillings are the most popular in Hungary.

The Dobos torte is a much-copied, many-layered cake invented by a famous Hungarian chef. The basis is a simple spongecake baked in thin layers. Between these is spread chocolate cream filling and the top is glazed with caramelized sugar. Other sponge-cakes are baked in thicker layers and may have any of a variety of fillings—almond or hazelnut cream, fruited whipped cream, chocolate or poppy seed.

The story goes that the apothecaries who came to the country with Queen Beatrix used to "gild" the *torta*—or decorate the cake—for festive occasions.

One delightful Christmas cake is made jelly-roll-fashion with filling between. Called *mákos és diós kalács* (poppy seed and nut cake), it is a yeast cake rich with butter. It will keep tender and delicious for a week or more. *Kis sütemény* (teacakes) are really cookies—buttery, sweet, fragile.

Coffeecakes made of yeast doughs are everyday treats in Hungary. Nuts, poppy seeds, and butter give them an irresistible fragrance and flavor. It is no wonder that *foszlós kalács* (flaky cake) is eaten warm. It would never last long enough to grow cool!

Strudels

STRUDEL DOUGH

RÉTESTÉSZTA

Members of the family, where strudel making is an art, eagerly watch the stretching of the tissue-thin dough. It is a fascinating procedure. Filled with fragrant fruit, nuts, cheese, or cabbage, strudel for dessert is a Sunday treat or a joyful surprise whenever the cook is inspired to test her skill.

2 cups sifted bread flour
1 tablespoon melted fat
¼ teaspoon salt
1 egg, separated
1 tablespoon vinegar
½ cup lukewarm water
¼ cup melted butter

ABOUT 20 SERVINGS

Make a hollow in the bowl of flour. Put in all the ingredients except the melted butter and egg white. Mix into a soft sticky dough. Knead, work, and pound it on the board until it is elastic and forms blisters as it is handled. It must lose all stickiness. Divide, and knead again into 2 perfect unbroken balls. Dust with flour and cover each ball with a warm mixing bowl. Let rest for 30 minutes.

Cover a table with a cloth and dust it with flour. Put a ball of dough in the center. Brush it with melted butter. Roll out till it is about ½ inch thick.

Brush again with melted butter. Now place fingers under the edge of the dough and gently stretch it in all directions toward the edge of the table. Lift and ease the dough carefully, always with hands under it to prevent breaks. When the dough is paper-thin—"thin enough to see through"—pull off the thicker edges. (These may be used later as noodles.) Let dry for 15 minutes.

Then sprinkle with melted butter and scatter on any desired filling. Lift one side of the cloth, thus tipping over an edge of the dough. With this fold start the roll. Continue rolling loosely, keeping the filling between the layers.

Butter a long baking pan. Cut the roll into lengths to fit and carefully lift it into the pan. Brush with egg white, and bake in a hot oven (450° F.) for about 35 minutes, or until crisp and brown. Repeat with the other half of the dough.

ALMOND STRUDEL

MANDULÁSRÉTES

10 SERVINGS

6 tablespoons sugar
6 eggs, separated
Grated rind of ½ lemon
Grated rind of ½ orange
¾ cup ground blanched almonds
2 tablespoons melted butter
½ recipe stretched Strudel Dough

Blend the sugar and egg yolks. Add the orange and lemon rind and the almonds. Mix well. Beat the egg whites stiff and fold into the yolk mixture. Spread over the thin sheet of dough, which has been brushed with the butter. Roll loosely, to allow space for the beaten eggs to expand during the baking. Cut the roll into lengths to fit a buttered pan, and bake in a hot oven (450° F.) for about 30 minutes, or until crisp and brown.

APPLE STRUDEL

ALMÁSRÉTES

10 TO 12 SERVINGS

½ recipe stretched Strudel Dough
¼ cup melted butter
¾ cup crushed walnuts
½ cup fine roll or bread crumbs
2 pounds apples, pared, thinly sliced
¾ cup sugar
¼ cup raisins

Sprinkle the thin sheet of dough with the butter. Mix the walnuts and crumbs, and spread over the surface. Combine raisins, apples and sugar, and scatter over all. Roll up the dough and cut into lengths to fit a long buttered pan. Bake in a hot oven (450° F.) for 40 minutes, or until crisp and brown.

CHERRY STRUDEL

CSERESZNYÉS RÉTES

½ recipe stretched Strudel Dough
2 tablespoons melted butter
½ cup sifted roll or bread crumbs
½ cup crushed almonds
1½ cups dark, sweet cherries, pitted
1 cup sugar
4 tablespoons sour cream

10 TO 12 SERVINGS

Brush the stretched dough with the butter and sprinkle with the crumbs. Scatter the almonds over all. Distribute the cherries evenly and sift the sugar over them. Roll up the dough. This requires care to keep the cherries from falling out. Cut the roll into lengths to fit a long buttered pan. Brush the roll with the sour cream and bake in a hot oven (450° F.) for about 40 minutes, or until crisp and brown.

CABBAGE STRUDEL

KÁPOSZTÁSRÉTES

5 cups grated cabbage
2 tablespoons salt
3 tablespoons sugar
4 tablespoons fat
1 teaspoon pepper
1 recipe stretched Strudel Dough
2 tablespoons melted butter

10 TO 12 SERVINGS

Stir the cabbage with the salt and let stand for 30 minutes. Squeeze out the moisture. Brown the sugar and the cabbage in the fat; cover, and cook until tender. Stir in the pepper, and cool thoroughly. Scatter evenly over the strudel dough, which has been brushed with the butter. Roll up, using care to keep the filling from falling out. Cut the completed roll into lengths to fit a buttered pan, and bake in a hot oven (450° F.) for about 25 minutes, or until crisp and brown.

CHEESE STRUDEL

TURÓSRÉTES

10 TO 12 SERVINGS

1 tablespoon butter
4 tablespoons sugar
4 eggs
1 pound cottage cheese, strained
3 tablespoons sour cream
⅓ cup seedless raisins
½ recipe stretched Strudel Dough
2 tablespoons melted butter

Cream the butter and sugar. Add the eggs and blend well. Mix in the cheese, sour cream, and raisins. Spread evenly over the strudel dough, which has been brushed with the melted butter. Roll up and cut into lengths to fit a buttered pan. Bake in a hot oven (450° F.) for about 40 minutes, or until crisp and brown.

CHEESE STRUDEL WITH DILL

KAPROS TURÓSRÉTES

This is a non-sweet strudel.

10 TO 12 SERVINGS

1 pound pot cheese, strained
2 eggs, separated
1 teaspoon salt
2 tablespoons chopped dill
4 tablespoons sour cream
½ recipe stretched Strudel Dough
2 tablespoons melted butter

Blend the cheese, egg yolks, salt, and dill. Beat the egg whites stiff and fold into the cheese mixture with the sour cream. Spread over the strudel dough, which has been brushed with the melted butter. Roll up loosely, to allow the beaten eggs to expand while baking. Cut the roll into lengths to fit a buttered pan. Bake in a hot oven (450° F.) until crisp and brown.

NUT STRUDEL

DIÓSRÉTES

10 TO 12 SERVINGS

1 cup ground nuts
1 cup sugar
½ cup milk
Grated rind of ½ lemon
½ cup seedless raisins
½ recipe stretched Strudel Dough
2 tablespoons melted butter

Cook the nuts, sugar, and milk together in a double boiler until slightly thickened. Add the lemon rind and raisins; mix and cool. Spread over the strudel dough, which has been brushed with the melted butter. Roll up, using care to keep the filling from falling out. Cut the completed roll into lengths to fit a buttered pan and bake in a hot oven (450° F.) for about 25 minutes, or until crisp and brown.

POPPY SEED STRUDEL

MÁKOSRÉTES

10 TO 12 SERVINGS

1 pound freshly ground poppy seeds
½ cup sugar
Grated rind of ½ lemon
½ cup milk
⅓ cup raisins or 2 apples, chopped
½ recipe stretched Strudel Dough
2 tablespoons melted butter

Cook the poppy seeds, sugar, grated lemon rind, and milk in a double boiler until slightly thickened. Add the raisins or apples; mix and cool. Spread on the strudel dough, which has been brushed with the butter. Roll up, using care to keep the filling from falling out. Cut the roll into lengths to fit a buttered pan, and bake in a hot oven (450° F.) for about 30 minutes, or until crisp and brown.

Pastries

MANY-LAYERED CAKE

DOBOS TORTA

This is the cake that was created when a famous Hungarian pastry chef named Dobos was challenged by his employer to make a cake very different from all others, very rich and so superior to other desserts that the confectionery store and the chef's skill would become famous all over the country. The Dobos torte was the result, and it became an immediate success. Its creator died in 1924, but the fame of his many-layered cake, with chocolate cream filling and a glaze of caramelized sugar, lives on, unexcelled. It requires a little patience to make this delicacy, but the directions are simple and the result a "dream" worth the trouble. It is better on the second day, and as good on the fifth—if ever it lasts that long.

5 eggs, separated
½ cup sugar
⅛ teaspoon salt
½ cup sifted flour

8 TO 10 SERVINGS

Beat the egg whites until stiff. Using the unwashed beater, beat the egg yolks, sugar, and salt until mixture thickens. Fold this into the beaten egg whites; then gradually fold in the flour, a little at a time. Bake 7 or 8 thin layers in pans first buttered, then lined with heavy paper. (Plain paper is better than waxed paper.) Spread ¼ inch of batter in each pan, and bake 10 minutes in a hot oven (400° F.). When cakes are done, they should be only lightly browned. Turn out and gently remove the paper at once.

CHOCOLATE CREAM FILLING

¼ pound (½ bar) semi-sweet chocolate, melted
6 eggs
1¾ cups sugar
1 cup butter

Beat the eggs and 1 cup of the sugar in the top of the double boiler and cook, stirring constantly, until mixture is thick. Remove from the heat and mix in the chocolate. Beat until cool, then thoroughly blend in all but 1 tablespoon of the butter.

Put the layers together with this cream filling, reserving enough to spread the sides of the finished cake. Leave off the top layer until glazed.

GLAZING

Melt the remaining sugar and the 1 tablespoon butter in a small pan; stir until golden, then quickly pour and spread over the single, top layer, which has been kept separate. Let cool a minute. Then with a thin knife, dipped in hot water, divide the cake into as many wedges as desired when the cake is cut. (This is necessary because the glaze hardens and cutting it on the cake would crush the layers.) Carefully place the wedges on the cake. Cover the sides of all layers with the reserved cream filling and store in the refrigerator.

SPONGECAKE

PISKÓTATÉSZTA

8 SERVINGS

6 eggs, separated
1 tablespoon lemon juice
1 cup sugar
1 cup flour

Beat the egg whites until stiff but not dry; then beat in about half the sugar. Using the same beater, beat egg yolks and lemon juice until thick and lemon-colored. Carefully fold into the egg whites. Mix the flour with the remaining sugar, and fold gradually into the egg mixture. Scrape down the sides of the bowl occasionally. Pour mixture into an ungreased loaf or tube pan. Bake in a moderately hot oven (375° F.) about 35 minutes, or until a light touch leaves no depression. Invert and allow to cool before loosening from the pan.

SPONGECAKE WITH FRUITED WHIPPED CREAM

PISKÓTATÉSZTA GYÜMÖLCSHABBAL

8 TO 10 SERVINGS

Spongecake
1 cup rum
½ cup heavy cream
¼ cup chopped candied fruit
½ cup fruit jam
¼ cup blanched, crushed almonds

Bake the Spongcake in a ring mold. Turn out on a cake platter. Cool. Pour rum over cake. Whip the cream, fold in fruit, and pile into the center of the cake. Spread thinly with jam and sprinkle with almonds. Chill in the refrigerator until time to serve.

SPONGECAKE WITHOUT SUGAR

PISKÓTATEKERCS CUKOR NÉLKÜL

8 TO 10 SERVINGS

6 eggs, separated
½ teaspoon salt
½ cup flour
½ cup grated soft American cheese

Beat the egg whites with the salt until they stand in stiff peaks. Beat the yolks until thick and lemon-colored. Fold into whites; then fold in the flour. Spread ½ inch thick in well-greased baking pans. Bake 15 minutes in a slow oven (325° F.). Turn out on a moist napkin, quickly spread with the cheese, and roll like a jelly roll. Return to the oven for 5 minutes, if the cheese does not soften. Serve in thin slices.

TOASTED HAZELNUT CAKE

PIRITOTT MOGYORÓTORTA

6 TO 8 SERVINGS

¼ cup butter
½ cup sugar
8 eggs, separated
¼ pound (½ bar) semi-sweet chocolate
½ cup fine roll or bread crumbs
½ cup toasted, ground hazelnuts

Beat together the butter, sugar, and egg yolks until mixture is thick and lemon-colored. Soften the chocolate in waxed paper over hot water. Stir the chocolate, crumbs, and nuts into the egg-yolk mixture. Beat the egg whites stiff and fold into the batter. Spread in 3 paper-lined layer pans and bake in a slow oven (325° F.) for 30 minutes, or until a light touch leaves no depression. Turn out one layer on a cake plate and remove the paper. Spread with Hazelnut Cream Filling and top with the next layer. (Remove paper *after* the layer is in place.) Spread the filling and continue with the last layer.

HAZELNUT CREAM FILLING

1 cup sugar
4 eggs
1 cup butter
¼ cup toasted, ground hazelnuts

Beat sugar and eggs in top of double boiler, cooking mixture until thick. Remove from heat, cool, then beat in the butter and nuts. Use as filling and topping for the cake.

POPPY SEED TORTE

MÁKTORTA

6 TO 8 SERVINGS

¼ cup butter
½ cup sugar
6 eggs, separated
½ cup fine roll or bread crumbs
¼ pound (½ bar) semi-sweet chocolate, melted
⅓ cup ground poppy seeds

Cream together the butter and sugar. Beat the egg whites stiff; then transfer the beater to the egg yolks, and beat them until thick and lemon-colored. Beat in the butter-sugar mixture and the crumbs. Fold chocolate into the egg-yolk mixture. Fold in the poppy seeds and the beaten egg whites. Spread in 2 paper-lined buttered layer pans, and bake in a slow oven (325° F.) for 30 minutes, or until a light touch leaves no depression. Turn out cake and remove the paper at once.

Note: The layers may be put together with strawberry or apricot jam. Cover the top and sides with Chocolate Cream Filling.

CHOCOLATE ALMOND TORTE

MANDULÁS CSOKOLÁDÉTORTA

8 TO 10 SERVINGS

8 eggs, separated
1 cup sugar
¼ pound (½ bar) semi-sweet chocolate
½ cup fine bread crumbs
1 cup blanched, crushed almonds
1 cup apricot jam

Beat together the egg yolks and sugar until mixture is thick and lemon-colored. Soften the chocolate on waxed paper over hot water and stir it, with the crumbs and almonds, into the egg-yolk mixture. Beat the egg whites until stiff, and fold into the yolk mixture. Spread in 3 buttered, paper-lined layer pans. Bake in a slow oven (325° F.) for 30 minutes, or until a light touch leaves no depression. Turn out and remove paper at once. Put layers together with a filling of apricot jam, and cover with Coffee Cream Frosting.

COFFEE CREAM FROSTING

6 eggs
⅓ cup strong coffee
¾ cup sugar
1 cup sweet butter

Cook together, in the top of a double boiler, the eggs, coffee, and sugar, stirring constantly until mixture thickens. Cool completely; then add butter and beat until thick enough to spread. Cover sides and top of cake.

CREAM PUFFS

KÉPVISELŐFÁNK

Hungarian housewives are devoted pastry makers and will spend hours beating, chilling, and baking cream puffs made with only the yolks of the eggs. A variation is suggested which uses the whole eggs and is quickly made with excellent results.

⅓ cup butter
⅔ cup milk
⅔ cup flour
½ teaspoon salt
6 egg yolks
½ cup heavy cream (for filling)

12 PUFFS

Heat the butter and milk in the top of a double boiler. Stir in the flour and salt, all at once, and continue to stir and beat until the mixture leaves the sides of the pan clean and forms a ball. Remove from the heat, cool slightly, then stir in 1 egg yolk at a time, beating vigorously after each addition. The final mixture should be glossy and smooth.

Chill for 1 hour. Then place heaping tablespoonfuls of the dough 4 inches apart on a greased baking sheet and bake in a very hot oven (550° F.) for 10 minutes. Without opening the oven door, reduce the heat to 450° F. for 10 minutes, then to 350° F. for 10 minutes more.

Cool the puffs and decorate with caramelized sugar syrup made by lightly browning about ¼ cup of sugar. Pour quickly over puffs, as it hardens almost at once. Fill with sweetened whipped cream just before serving.

Variation: Use 4 whole eggs instead of 6 yolks. Omit the cooling and chilling and bake as soon as mixture is blended with the eggs. Bake in a hot oven

(450° F.) for 35 to 40 minutes, or until puffs are lightly browned.

COFFEECAKE

BÁBA KALÁCS

This is a Transylvanian specialty—a kind of sponge coffeecake served with afternoon coffee.

½ package granular yeast
2 tablespoons lukewarm water
¼ cup white sugar
¼ cup butter
½ teaspoon salt
⅔ cup lukewarm milk
6 egg yolks
2 cups flour
½ cup coarsely chopped nuts
½ cup brown sugar
1 teaspoon vanilla

8 SERVINGS

Soak the yeast in the water for 15 minutes. Then stir in the white sugar, butter, salt, milk, and egg yolks. Add half the flour and beat vigorously until smooth. Cover mixture and leave in a warm place for 30 minutes. Meanwhile combine the nuts, brown sugar, and vanilla. Now stir the remainder of the flour into the batter, making a soft, spongy dough that can be dropped from a spoon. Stir until it becomes elastic and blisters.

Spoon half the dough into a well-greased ring mold. Sprinkle with half the nut mixture. Add the rest of the dough and top with the nut mixture. Cover with a towel and leave in a warm place until dough doubles in bulk. Bake in a moderate oven (350° F.) for 45 minutes, or until golden brown.

POPPY SEED BALLS

MÁKOSGUBÓ

This is a favorite Christmas Eve dessert. Prepare raised dough according to the preceding recipe, and cut it into pieces the size of a hazelnut. Shape into balls, roll in flour, and space in a baking pan so they do not touch. Let rise 30 minutes. Bake in a very slow oven (250° F.) until they are faintly browned, about 1 hour. Remove from oven and pour boiling water over them. Stir them in the water. Then quickly pour it off. Heat ¼ cup of butter in a large skillet. Turn the moistened rolls into it and stir until coated with the butter. Then sprinkle generously with equal parts of crushed poppy seeds and sugar, until each roll is well covered.

40 TO 50 ROLLS

COTTAGE CHEESE CAKE

TURÓSLEPÉNY

1 pound cottage cheese
4 eggs, separated
1 cup sugar
⅛ teaspoon salt
Grated rind of 1 lemon
1 tablespoon lemon juice
2 teaspoons farina
1 cup heavy cream
9-inch pastry shell, lightly baked
Strips of unbaked pastry

6 SERVINGS

Press the cheese through a sieve. Beat the egg yolks until they are thick and lemon-colored. Beat in the sugar, salt, lemon rind and juice, and the farina. Combine with the cheese and blend well. Whip the cream and fold it into the cheese mixture. Fill the pastry shell. Arrange narrow strips of thinly rolled pastry over the top, and bake in slow oven (300° F.) for 40 minutes, or until set.

Note: This mixture is often made as a cake in a square baking pan which has been lined with sweetened, buttered roll crumbs.

FLAKY CAKE

FOSZLÓS KALÁCS

10 TO 12 SERVINGS

1 package granular yeast
1 cup lukewarm milk
½ cup sugar
1½ teaspoons salt
3 egg yolks
4 cups flour
⅔ cup butter

Soak the yeast for 15 minutes in ¼ cup of the milk with 1 teaspoon of the sugar. Combine the rest of the milk, half the remaining sugar, the salt, and the egg yolks. Beat vigorously. Stir in half the flour. Add the yeast mixture and continue stirring and beating until dough is smooth and elastic. Mix in the rest of the flour and beat again. Stir in ½ cup of the butter, a tablespoonful at a time, mixing well after each addition. Cover dough and set it in a warm place to rise for 1 hour. Then make it into 2 loaves. Flatten each, and stretch until about 1 inch thick.

Melt the remaining butter and spread over the dough. Sprinkle with the rest of the sugar, and roll each loaf like a jelly roll. Flatten one end of each roll, and join the flattened ends together. Twist the ends in opposite directions. Then twine the coil together to form a rope of dough. Place in a round baking pan and let rise until double in size. Bake in a moderate oven (350° F.) for 30 minutes, or until cake is brown and firm to the touch. To serve, tear apart rather than cut.

ALMOND ROLLS

MANDULÁSTEKERCS

20 SERVINGS

1 cup milk
1 package granular yeast
⅓ cup white sugar
1½ teaspoons salt
4 eggs or 8 egg yolks, beaten
⅓ cup butter
4 cups sifted flour
1 cup chopped almonds
1 cup brown sugar

Heat the milk to boiling, then cool to lukewarm. Pour a fourth of it over the yeast. Add 1 teaspoon of the sugar and let mixture stand about 15 minutes. Combine the rest of the white sugar, the milk, salt, eggs, and all but about 1 tablespoon of the butter. Blend well. Add half the flour and beat until smooth. Add the remaining flour and mix until elastic. Turn out on a floured board and knead until velvety smooth. Place in a greased bowl and set in a warm place to rise for 30 minutes.

Mix the almonds and brown sugar. Melt the reserved butter. Turn the dough onto a floured board, divide in half, and roll to "knife-blade thinness." Brush each with the melted butter, and cover with some of the almond mixture. Roll up jelly-roll-fashion. Place in a long baking pan, sprinkle with remaining almonds, and set in a warm place to rise until double in size. Bake in a slow oven (325° F.) until golden brown, about 35 minutes. Cool slightly before slicing.

TEACAKES OR COOKIES

KIS SÜTEMÉNY

100 OR MORE

4 cups flour
1 cup sweet butter
1¼ cups sugar
½ teaspoon salt
4 eggs, separated
2 tablespoons heavy cream
2 teaspoons vanilla
½ cup chopped walnuts or almonds

With the fingers, blend the flour, butter, 1 cup of the sugar, and the salt. Add the egg yolks, cream, and vanilla and mix to make a pliable dough. Roll out ¼ inch thick and cut into fancy shapes. Beat the egg whites lightly and brush the cookies with them. Mix the walnuts with the remaining sugar and sprinkle over the cookies. Bake on a greased cooky sheet in a moderate oven (350° F.) until golden, about 10 minutes.

Note: When the cookies are cool, they may be put together with apricot jam.

CHESTNUT BALLS

GESZTENYEGOLYÓK

ABOUT 50 BALLS

1 pound chestnuts
2 cups granulated sugar
¼ cup water
½ cup confectioners' sugar

Boil the chestnuts, remove the skins, and press the meat through a strainer. Boil the granulated sugar and water to make a very thick syrup—till a few drops form brittle beads in cold water. Combine with the chestnuts. When the mixture is cool enough to handle, form small balls and drop them into a paper bag containing the confectioners' sugar. Shake the bag to coat the candy.

POPPY SEED AND NUT CAKES

MÁKOS ÉS DIÓS KALÁCS

These favorite cakes are awaited with great expectancy at Christmastime.

20 SERVINGS

½ package granular yeast
1 teaspoon sugar
⅔ cup lukewarm milk
2¼ cups flour
1 cup butter
¼ cup sugar
½ teaspoon salt
Grated rind of 1 lemon
1 egg, slightly beaten

Soak the yeast and the teaspoon of sugar in the milk. With the fingers blend together the flour, butter, sugar, salt, and lemon rind. When the yeast is softened and the mixture has bubbles, work it into the dough. Knead well, then divide into two greased bowls, cover with a towel, and set in a warm place to rise for 1 hour.

Then roll out ¼ inch thick. Spread with the Poppy Seed Filling, which follows, and roll like a jelly roll. Place in a greased pan, brush with the egg, and let rise for 30 minutes. Again brush with egg, prick well with a needle to prevent blistering, and bake in a slow oven (325° F.) for 45 minutes, or until lightly browned.

POPPY SEED FILLING

MÁKTÖLTELÉK

½ pound poppy seeds, ground
1 cup sugar

Grated rind of 1 lemon
½ cup raisins
½ cup milk

Combine ingredients in the top of a double boiler and cook over boiling water until thick enough to spread easily on the unbaked dough.

Note: Ground walnuts instead of poppy seeds may be used for this filling.

DEVIL'S PILLS

ÖRDÖGPIRULÁK

1 cup sugar
2 tablespoons orange juice
Grated rind of 2 oranges
1 cup blanched and toasted crushed almonds
½ cup chopped candied fruit
½ cup grated bitter chocolate

ABOUT 25

Melt the sugar with the orange juice and rind. Add the almonds and the fruit. Form small balls and roll in the grated chocolate.

HUSSAR'S KISSES

HUSZÁRCSÓK

1½ cups flour
¾ cup soft butter
½ cup sugar
Grated rind of 1 lemon
1 egg, separated
½ cup chopped almonds
½ cup thick jam

20 TO 30 KISSES

Blend the flour, butter, sugar, lemon rind, and egg yolk. Make small balls; dip each in egg white and roll in chopped almonds. Place on a greased baking sheet. Make a depression in each ball and bake in a moderately hot oven (375° F.) until lightly browned. Fill the depressions with jam.

WALNUT KISSES

DIÓS CSÓK

ABOUT 30 KISSES

4 egg whites, beaten stiff
1½ cups sugar
1 tablespoon lemon juice
1½ cups chopped walnuts

In the top of a double boiler combine the egg whites, sugar, and lemon juice, and beat constantly over hot water for 10 minutes. Add the nuts. Drop by spoonfuls onto a greased baking sheet. Bake in a slow oven (325° F.) until lightly browned. Remove from the baking sheet while they are still warm.

DESSERTS

DESSERTS

In Hungary, fruit, abundant and unrivaled in flavor and aroma, is served at any time during the meal. With the meat course a dish of fruit is frequently served if there is not a specific fruit sauce—of, say, raspberries or gooseberries. The plentiful supply makes home canning a necessity. Later the mellow preserved fruit is served with pride and pleasure as a compote at the close of a meal. Fresh or canned, with cheese or alone, fruit makes a pleasant end to many a meal, though it is hardly thought of as a dessert. Fruit is also an essential ingredient of the tempting pastry delicacies produced in Magyar kitchens.

The variety of Hungarian desserts is endless. The lighter soufflés and puddings, rich in eggs, are prepared for the sick but enjoyed equally by those "in the pink." The best-loved desserts are those of the dumpling or noodle variety. Plum dumplings are the everyday favorite. So are the cabbage, nut, poppy seed, and cottage cheese noodles.

The fun of making some of the specialty sweets such as fried cherries, golden dumplings, fried sweet noodles, rose fritters, or little baskets is exceeded only by the enormous pleasure of feasting on them!

STEAMED CHOCOLATE SOUFFLÉ

CSOKOLÁDÉFELFUJT

6 SERVINGS

6 eggs, separated
½ cup grated semi-sweet chocolate
1 teaspoon cocoa
½ cup granulated sugar
3 tablespoons roll or bread crumbs
1 cup heavy cream, whipped

Beat the egg whites stiff. Transfer the beater to egg yolks, add sugar, and beat until thick and lemon-colored. Add 1 tablespoon crumbs, the cocoa, and the finely grated chocolate. Fold egg whites into mixture. Butter the top of a double boiler and coat with crumbs. Pour in the prepared mixture and steam over gently boiling water for 1 hour. Serve with whipped cream.

STEAMED POT CHEESE SOUFFLÉ

TURÓSFELFUJT

6 SERVINGS

6 eggs, separated
¼ cup sugar
¼ cup softened butter
½ cup pot cheese
1 tablespoon potato flour
¼ cup blanched crushed almonds
¼ cup currants, washed and dried
Grated rind of 1 lemon
1 tablespoon butter
2 tablespoons roll or bread crumbs

Beat the egg whites stiff. Transfer the beater to the egg yolks; add sugar and beat until thick and lemon-colored. Beat in the ¼ cup butter and the cheese. Stir in the flour, almonds, currants, and lemon rind. Fold in the beaten egg whites. Butter the top of a double boiler and coat it with the crumbs. Pour in the soufflé mixture, cover, and steam over gently boiling water for 1 hour. Serve warm.

STEAMED APRICOT SOUFFLÉ

BARACKFELFUJT

Dedicated to Mary Margaret McBride, who considers it "my favorite dessert in all the world . . . almost the most beautiful dish you could ever see."

1 cup dried apricots
½ cup water
6 eggs, separated
¼ cup sugar
1 tablespoon potato flour
1 tablespoon butter
2 tablespoons roll or bread crumbs
Blanched ground almonds
Whipped cream

6 SERVINGS

Cook the apricots in water until all water is absorbed, being careful not to scorch. Press through a strainer and cool. (Or use apricot jam.)

Beat the egg whites stiff. Transfer the beater to the egg yolks; add the sugar and beat until thick and lemon-colored. Blend in the cold apricots. Fold in the beaten egg whites and the flour. Butter the top of a double boiler, and coat it with the crumbs. Pour in the soufflé mixture, cover, and cook over gently boiling water. Do not lift the lid until 1 hour has passed. Serve at once, garnished with almonds and whipped cream.

Note: Some cooks prefer to put the

soufflé in a baking dish and bake it slowly in the oven. Set the dish in a pan of water while baking to prevent the soufflé from collapsing when removed from the oven. Bake in a slow oven (325° F.) and allow ½ hour before testing. The soufflé may have a light brown tint.

APRICOT CREAM

BARACKKRÉM

6 SERVINGS

- *8 fresh ripe apricots or ½ cup dried apricots*
- *½ tablespoon gelatin*
- *½ cup sugar*
- *2 tablespoons lemon juice*
- *1 cup heavy cream, whipped*

Peel the fresh or cook the dried apricots, and press through a strainer. Dissolve the gelatin and sugar in the lemon juice over hot water. Blend with the apricot pulp. Chill in refrigerator until jelling starts, about 45 minutes. Then fold apricot mixture into whipped cream and chill until time to serve. It may be piled into individual serving dishes before second chilling.

CHESTNUT CREAM

GESZTENYEKRÉM

6 SERVINGS

- *1 pound chestnuts, mashed*
- *6 egg yolks*
- *⅓ cup sugar*
- *1 cup milk*
- *2 tablespoons rum*
- *1 cup heavy cream*

Boil the chestnuts in water, remove the skins, and press the meat through a strainer. In the top of a double boiler, over low heat, stir the egg yolks, sugar, and milk until thick and smooth. Mix in the chestnut purée. Cool, then stir in the rum. An hour before serving, whip the cream and fold it into the chilled cooked mixture. Pile into individual serving dishes and chill.

BAKED APPLE WITH WINE SAUCE

SÜLT ALMA BORMÁRTÁSSAL

6 SERVINGS

6 baking apples
6 tablespoons sugar
6 tablespoons strawberry or apricot jam
½ cup chopped walnuts

Wash and core the apples and score the skin around the apple about ½ inch down from the top of each one. Place in a baking pan; put 1 tablespoon sugar in the center of each and bake in a moderately hot oven (375° F.) until apples are tender but not falling apart, about 40 minutes. Mix the jam and walnuts and fill the apple centers. Chill and serve with Wine Sauce.

CORN MEAL MUSH WITH COTTAGE CHEESE

PULISZKA

8 SERVINGS

4 cups boiling water
1½ cups corn meal
1½ teaspoons salt
2 cups cottage or grated cheese
¼ cup butter, melted

Into the boiling water gradually stir the corn meal. Add salt, and continue to boil gently until very thick. Pour a thick layer of the mush about 1 inch thick into a buttered baking dish. Spread with a ½-inch-thick layer of cheese and sprinkle with melted butter. Add another layer of mush, and continue until all the cheese is used. End with mush and sprinkle with the butter. Bake in a moderately hot oven (375° F.) for about 30 minutes, or until slightly browned. Turn out onto a warm platter to serve.

CORN MEAL MUSH WITH CREAM

BÁLMOS

This is a Transylvanian specialty—a great favorite for supper in the sheep-raising areas. Sometimes it is made with buffalo cream or whey left over from cheese making.

4 cups heavy cream
1 teaspoon salt
2 cups yellow corn meal
grated cheese

8 SERVINGS

Heat the cream to boiling and add the salt. Gradually stir in the corn meal, keeping the cream at boiling point. Cook, stirring constantly, for about 30 minutes. As mixture thickens, butter fat from the cream will become visible. Spoon the thick mush onto a platter, arranging it in dumpling-like mounds around the edge of the dish. Pour the butter fat in the center. Serve very hot, sprinkled with grated cheese.

NOODLE "DOUGHNUTS"

METÉLT FÁNK

1 whole egg
2 egg yolks
½ teaspoon salt

2 cups flour
3 cups milk
½ cup blanched crushed almonds
½ cup granulated sugar
½ teaspoon vanilla
2 eggs, slightly beaten
1 cup bread crumbs
½ cup fat
½ cup confectioners' sugar

6 TO 8 SERVINGS

Mix the egg, egg yolks, and salt into the flour, making a dry dough. Roll out very thin, and cut into broad noodles. Boil the noodles in the milk until all moisture is absorbed. Stir in the almonds, granulated sugar, and vanilla. While still hot, pack ½ inch thick into a buttered baking pan. Cool. Turn out on a board and cut into circles with a cooky cutter. Dip each round in egg, then in crumbs. Fry in hot fat. Sprinkle with confectioners' sugar and set in a warm oven until all the "doughnuts" are fried. Serve hot.

CARNIVAL DOUGHNUTS

FARSANGI FÁNK

1 package granular yeast
2 cups lukewarm milk
1 tablespoon sugar
½ cup butter
5 egg yolks, slightly beaten
1 teaspoon salt
5 cups sifted flour
Hot fat
Vanilla-flavored sugar

ABOUT 25 DOUGHNUTS

Soak the yeast with the sugar in ¼ cup of the milk for about 15 minutes. Melt the butter in the remaining warm milk. Combine milk with the egg yolks, salt, and the yeast mixture. Stir in half the flour and beat well. Mix in the remaining flour and stir or knead until the soft dough is elastic and smooth. Place in a greased bowl, cover, and let rise in a warm place until double in bulk, about 45 minutes. Roll out ½ inch thick and cut into doughnuts, and fry in hot fat until golden, turning once to brown both sides. Dust with sugar, which has been stored overnight with a vanilla bean in a closed container. Serve hot.

CRISP OR CURLED FRITTERS

CSÖRÖGE OR FORGÁCSFÁNK

6 TO 8 SERVINGS

3 egg yolks
3 tablespoons cream
½ teaspoon salt
1 tablespoon granulated sugar
6 tablespoons rum
2 cups flour
Hot fat
½ cup confectioners' sugar

Combine the egg yolks, cream, salt, granulated sugar, and rum. Mix these into the flour and knead until mixture no longer sticks to the board. Let stand for 20 minutes, then roll out ⅛ inch thick. Cut into strips 6 inches x 1 inch, tie in a loose knot, and fry in deep fat. Sprinkle with confectioners' sugar. Serve hot.

ROSE FRITTERS

RÓZSA FÁNK

Make the dough as in the preceding recipe. Then cut with 3 different-sized cooky cutters. Brush a bit of unbeaten egg white over the center of the largest circles. Place the medium-size circles on the large ones and brush the centers with egg white. Top with the smallest circles. Press gently in the center to seal the layers. Then, with a spatula, lift each stack into deep fat. Fry only a few at a time. When lightly browned, remove and sprinkle with a little confectioners' sugar. The layers will curl in the hot fat and give the effect of a rose. Place a bit of raspberry jam in center of rose.

FRIED SWEET NOODLES

CSURGATOTT TÉSZTA

This intriguing dessert is a Hungarian favorite—and it will be yours.

2½ cups flour
½ cup granulated sugar
½ teaspoon salt
1 cup milk
1 cup sweet wine
8 eggs
Hot fat
¼ cup confectioners' sugar
Jam (optional)

8 SERVINGS

Combine the flour, granulated sugar, and salt. Add the milk and half the wine; stir until smooth. Stir in the rest of the wine and the eggs.

Make a funnel of brown paper, fastening it with scotch tape and leaving a very small opening at the tip. In a deep kettle, heat the fat until a drop of batter browns in 1 minute. Partially fill the funnel with batter, then move it in circles over the hot fat, letting the batter run in a small stream. The "noodles" formed in the fat should not stick together or become brown. As they turn yellow and start to brown, lift them out by winding them around a fork. Arrange in little piles on a serving plate. Dust with confectioners' sugar or jam, or both.

DEEP-FRIED CHERRIES

CSERESZNYE KISÜTVE

This unique dessert is eagerly awaited during cherry season.

1 cup flour
¼ cup granulated sugar
⅓ cup milk
½ cup wine
3 eggs, slightly beaten
1 pound ripe red cherries
½ cup confectioners' sugar
1 teaspoon cinnamon
Hot fat

6 SERVINGS

Mix the flour, granulated sugar, salt, milk, and wine to a smooth batter. Stir in the eggs. Dip a cluster of cherries into the batter—be sure all the cherries are well coated—then quickly plunge them into hot fat. When they are browned, remove with a skimmer. Sprinkle with the cinnamon and confectioners' sugar, which have been combined.

NOODLES-IN-MILK DESSERT

TEJBENFÖTT LASKA

¼ cup butter
4 cups milk
¼ cup granulated sugar
2 cups Noodles
¼ cup raisins

1 teaspoon vanilla

8 SERVINGS *¼ cup confectioners' sugar*

Melt the butter in the top of a large double boiler over direct heat. Add the milk and heat to boiling. Stir in the granulated sugar and Noodles, and cook over hot water until the Noodles are tender and the milk is absorbed. Occasional stirring may be necessary. Stir in the raisins and vanilla; then turn into a buttered baking dish. Bake in a hot oven (400° F.) until mixture is crisp on top and at sides. Turn out on a platter and dust with confectioners' sugar. Cut and serve pie-fashion.

SUGAR-GLAZED ALMONDS

GRILLÁZS

1 pound blanched and ground almonds
1 cup sugar

Heat together the almonds and sugar in a saucepan until light brown. Cool. Grind and use for topping on torten or other desserts.

POTATO NOODLES

BURGONYAMETÉLT

These noodles are a favorite dessert.

6 boiled potatoes, pared
1 egg
½ teaspoon salt
1½ cups sifted flour
1 cup fine bread crumbs
3 tablespoons butter

6 SERVINGS *¼ cup confectioners' sugar*

Press the potatoes through a strainer while they are warm. Blend with the egg and salt. Stir in the flour, adding more if needed to make a workable dough. Knead well, then make into sausage-like rolls. Cut into ½-inch pieces, roll into noodles, and cook 10 minutes in salted water. Meanwhile brown the crumbs in the butter. Drain the noodle pieces and coat them with the crumb mixture. Dust with the sugar and serve warm.

PLUM DUMPLINGS

SZILVÁSGOMBÓC

Hungarians have a great fondness for this dessert. The plums must be prepared before the dough.

12 plums
12 lumps of sugar
3 tablespoons butter
2 cups flour
2 cups riced, cooked potatoes, chilled
1 teaspoon salt
2 eggs
¾ cup buttered crumbs

6 SERVINGS

Remove the pits but do not cut the plums completely apart. Fill centers with the sugar.

Cut the butter into the flour, until mixture is like coarse corn meal. Combine it with the potatoes and salt. Mix in the eggs and knead the dough well. Roll out ¼ inch thick on a floured board. Cut into 3-inch squares. Place a prepared plum on each square. Moisten the edges of the dough and pinch it together around the plum. Dust the palms of the hands with flour and roll the dough into dumplings. Gently drop the dumplings into a large kettle of boiling water, a few at a time. The water must boil without stopping, but not too vigorously, or it will break the dumplings. Cook them for 15 minutes, then carefully lift each out and roll it in buttered crumbs. Serve hot.

POT CHEESE NOODLES

TURÓSCSUSZA

8 SERVINGS

1 recipe Noodle Dough, thinly rolled
½ pound bacon, chopped
1 cup sour cream
1 pound pot cheese

Tear the freshly made noodles into 1-inch pieces. Cook in salted water until tender. Fry the bacon until crisp and lift from fat. Pour out all but about 2 tablespoons of the fat. Roll the cooked drained noodles lightly in the fat. Stir in half the sour cream and cheese. Heat 1 minute, then turn out on a warm serving dish. Top with the remaining cheese and garnish with the rest of the cream and the bacon cracklings. Serve piping hot.

Note: Commercially prepared strip noodles may be used if preferred.

RUM BUTTER BISCUITS

VAJAS POGÁCSA

10 SERVINGS

½ cup butter
1 cup sifted flour
½ teaspoon salt
2 tablespoons rum
3 egg yolks

Cut the butter into the flour until there are granules the size of peas. Combine the salt, rum, and 2 of the egg yolks. Stir into the flour mixture. Knead lightly, then chill well. Roll out ¼-inch thick, cut into 2-inch rounds, and brush with the reserved egg yolk, slightly beaten. Bake in a moderate oven (350° F.) about 10 minutes, or until golden.

GOLDEN DUMPLINGS

ARANYGALUSKA

1 package granular yeast
¼ cup lukewarm water
2½ cups milk
2 tablespoons fat
¼ cup sugar
1 teaspoon salt
8 cups sifted flour
6 eggs
¼ cup melted butter

ABOUT 15 SERVINGS

FILLING

1 cup chopped blanched almonds
1 cup brown sugar
½ cup raisins

Mix the yeast with the water; let stand 15 minutes. Scald the milk; add the fat, sugar, and salt; then cool to lukewarm. Combine the flour, eggs, milk mixture, and yeast solution. Stir and beat the dough vigorously until it is smooth and elastic. Place in a greased bowl. Cover with waxed paper and a towel, and let stand in a warm place about 1 hour.

When the dough has doubled in bulk, turn it out on a floured board and knead until it is elastic. Pinch off small bits of the dough, about 1 inch across. Roll into balls.

Dip balls in melted butter and place close together in a deep, buttered baking pan. When one layer is formed, top it with half of the almond filling. Arrange the second layer and sprinkle the rest of the filling over it. The baking pan should be about half full. Let dough rise 15 minutes in a warm place, then set it in a slightly warm oven. Bake at 300° F. for 30 minutes, then increase the heat to 375° F. and bake until golden brown. Pull apart to serve.

LITTLE BASKETS

KOSÁRKÁK

American-Hungarians serve this as a party dessert, each trying to excel the other. It is an unforgettable delicacy.

12 TO 15 SERVINGS

⅔ cup butter
1 cup sifted flour
10 eggs, separated
1 cup sugar
1⅓ cups ground or crushed nuts
⅔ cup chocolate bits

Combine the butter and the flour. Blend in the egg yolks. Separate the mixture into nut-sized portions and chill for several hours. Shape each portion into a ball. Roll thin and fit into very small buttered pie tins or shallow custard cups. Beat the egg whites stiff and fold in the sugar, nuts, and chocolate. Fill the pastry-lined tins with this egg-white mixture. Bake in a moderate oven (350° F.) for 20 minutes, or until golden.

BEVERAGES

COFFEE

Coffee is the most important everyday beverage in Hungary but it is not served with every meal. For breakfast it is considered a necessity and is served "half and half"—half coffee and half boiled milk. Those who prefer it still mellower, top the coffee with the "creamy skin of the milk" and sweeten it freely with sugar.

Morning coffee is prepared from not too darkly roasted coffee beans with some chicory added, which gives it a darker hue. Afternoon coffee, served at four, is coffee as it is usually prepared for guests—from freshly roasted beans. The aroma from the roasting, incidentally, is part of the "treat." A smaller amount of boiled milk than is used in the morning is added and the cup is topped to overflowing with heavy whipped cream. Coffee is not always served with the noon meal or with supper. But after more formal evening dinners demitasse is served. The after-dinner coffee is a strong brew, again made from freshly roasted beans and without chicory.

Purchased green, even an inferior grade of coffee bean makes good coffee when freshly roasted and ground. Modest homes can thus enjoy fine coffee, by roasting and grinding their own.

CHOCOLATE, COCOA, AND TEA

Chocolate is used as a beverage of rich and substantial quality. It, too, appears with generous amounts of whipped cream, and is often served instead of coffee in the afternoon. In summer it is enjoyed cold; in the winter, hot.

Cocoa is prepared for children from hot milk and a paste of cocoa and sugar.

Tea is served with the "English"-type breakfast, and enjoys popularity with both men and women for five o'clock refreshment.

MINERAL WATER

Hungary is rich in mineral waters of excellent quality. Many are naturally effervescent. They are served chilled or on ice, but never mixed with ice. Those who can afford it serve mineral water with meals every day; others serve it to guests or on special occasions.

WINE, BRANDY, AND LIQUEURS

Wine, probably the most popular beverage in Hungary, mixes well with the sparkling mineral waters in a variety of drinks. These mixtures do not, however, displace straight wine as the delicate accompaniment of fine rich food. With soup, a *Szamorodni* wine may be served. Fish takes one of the lighter white wines, such as *Leányka* (little girl). This may be followed, during the meat course, by the stronger red wine, *Egri bikavér*, or one of the heavy white wines, such as *Badacsonyi szürke barát* (grey monk), or *Badacsonyi kéknyelű* (blue neck).

From the district of Tokaj (Tokay) comes the famous Tokaj wine. It was here that royalty and the nobility had their cellars. But the very best wines were produced in small places like Maád in the more carefully cultivated vineyards of small proprietors.

The preparation of the wine requires the most thoughtful care. The grape harvest begins in the last days of October, depending on the full ripeness of the grapes. These are left on the vine to shrivel into raisins (*Aszú Szöllő*) in order to achieve the fiery sweetness of the wine.

The harvest festivities are vividly described by Theresa Pulszky in her *Memoirs of a Hungarian Lady*, published in London in 1850. She recalls the bygone joys and entertainments on the

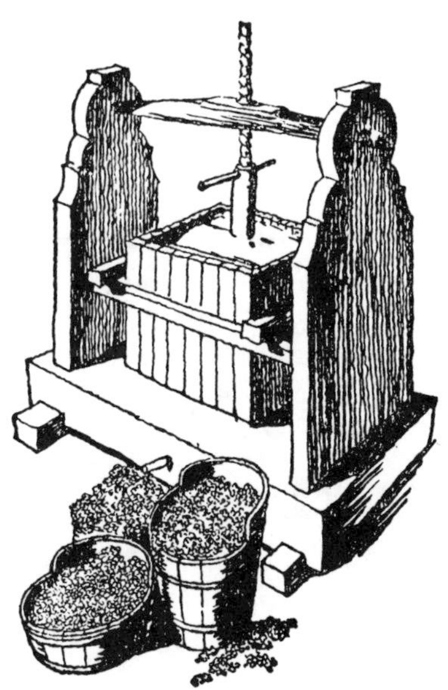

thirty-first day of October, 1845, in one of the most renowned vineyards in Maád. She says that both gentry and vintagers participated in their diligent gathering and eating of the grapes, while the ladies busied themselves with the preparation of the meal. They converted wine tubs into dinner tables, covered them with cloths, and transformed the smaller casks into seats. The food was profuse and the gypsy music made old and young dance around with great abandon. Even unfavorable weather could not greatly dim the gaiety of the occasion.

Known the world over is *barackpálinka* (apricot brandy). *Diópálinka* (walnut brandy), *szilvapálinka* (plum brandy), and *baracklikőr* (apricot liqueur) are also widely enjoyed.

COFFEE—HALF AND HALF

TEJESKÁVÉ

This "morning coffee," as it is called, is preferred for breakfast.

2 cups strong coffee
2 cups hot milk
Cream (optional)
Sugar

6 SERVINGS

Prepare a favorite brew of freshly roasted and ground coffee with 1 tablespoon chicory added. Serve it hot, along with a pitcher containing the boiled milk. Cream may be offered or omitted.

AFTERNOON COFFEE

UZSONNAKÁVÉ

3 cups strong coffee
1 cup hot milk
1 cup heavy cream, whipped

6 TO 8 SERVINGS

Prepare the favorite brew of freshly ground coffee with 2 tablespoons chicory added. Make it very strong and very hot. Add the hot milk. Heap the whipped cream on the cups of coffee, to the point of overflow.

DEMITASSE

FEKETEKÁVÉ

8 TO 10 SERVINGS

3 cups boiling water
8 tablespoons freshly ground coffee

Use a filter coffee-maker. Pour the boiling water over the coffee. Serve in small cups as soon as the brew is through the filter.

HOT CHOCOLATE WITH WHIPPED CREAM

MELEG CSOKOLÁDÉ TEJSZINHABBAL

8 SERVINGS

4-ounce sweet chocolate
1 quart milk
1 cup heavy cream
2 tablespoons sugar (optional)

Melt the chocolate over hot water, add 1 tablespoon of the milk, and blend well. Add the rest of the milk, stir, and heat to boiling. Whip the cream, add the sugar, and blend. Serve the chocolate very hot, topped with the whipped cream.

COCOA

KAKAÓ

6 SERVINGS

6 teaspoons cocoa
2 tablespoons cold water
8 teaspoons sugar
4 cups milk

Mix the cocoa and sugar in a pitcher. Add the cold water and blend. Heat the milk to boiling and stir it into the cocoa mixture.

BURNT PUNCH FOR NEW YEAR'S EVE

KRAMPAMPULI

On Sylvester night—New Year's Eve—this drink or champagne is preferred to all others.

1 cup chopped figs
1 cup chopped dates
1 cup chopped candied fruit peel
1 pound lump sugar
2 tablespoons grated orange rind
1 cup brandy or rum
4 cups wine
2 sticks cinnamon
Strips of lemon peel
2 cups hot tea
Juice of 2 lemons
Juice of 2 oranges

25 TO 30 SERVINGS

As midnight approaches, place a deep earthenware or glass baking dish in the center of the table. Into it put the figs, dates, and fruit peel. Place a meshed grill over fruit and pile sugar on it. Sprinkle with the orange rind, then with the brandy or rum. Let stand until all is absorbed by the sugar.

Put out the lights and, with a taper, light the brandy. While it burns, boil together on the stove the wine, cinnamon, and lemon peel. Remove cinnamon and peel. When the enchanting blue flame of the brandy has burned itself out, pour over the fruits the hot wine, tea, and fruit juices. Stir, and serve in punch glasses with some of the fruit in each one.

A GUIDE TO HUNGARIAN WINES

Some of the finest wines in the world are produced in Hungary, which has been recognized as a center of excellent wine-making for centuries. The Hungarian climate is very temperate and ideal for wine production, with more sunshine than western European countries in the same latitude. Wines produced in Hungary are made from local grapes as well as varieties of Austrian, French and Italian grapes.

Some Wine Regions

TOKAJ-HEGYALJA

The wines produced in this district are Hungary's most famous. The region is located in northeast Hungary, on the slopes of the Eperjes-Tokaj mountains, with an ideal southeastern outlook. The Tokaj-Hegyalja region includes all the wine produced in twenty-eight hill villages. The first part of the name is taken from the village *Tokaj* and the second part, *Hegyalja*, is the Magyar word for "foothill district." The climate is dry with hot summers, sunny extended autumns and cold stormy winters. The soil from which the famous Tokaj wines are made is volcanic andesite and rhyolite covered by decayed lava and loess.

The *Tokaj* region has been well-known since the time of the Celts. Around 1650, however, the secret of making the Aszú wine was discovered, and the wines of Tokaj achieved worldwide renown. A typical blend of grapes for a Tokaj wine would be:

Furmint	70%
Linden Leaf	20%
Yellow Muscat	5-10%

The essential conditions for production of the high quality Tokaj wines include ideal climate, suitable soils, cellars carved out of rock or dug out of loess for cool temperatures, and the unique flavor from the Gönc casks in which the wines are aged.

TOKAJI ASZÚ ESSENCIA

This is the hallmark white wine of the Tokaj region, known as "Vinum Regnum, Rex Vinorum" ("The Wine of Kings, the King of Wines"). It has the special Aszú bouquet and aroma which is produced from the fermentation of the must or wine added to the carefully selected Aszú grapes. This is a full-bodied and fairly rich table wine, sweet without being cloying, with a dry finish, and incomparable flavor and aroma.

BADACSONY

The Badacsony district consists of volcanic hills, whose heat-absorbing soil makes it a perfect site for wine-making. Many of the vineyards are situated on hillsides and receive the generous sunlight that is reflected off the waters of the northern shore of Lake Balaton.

SZÜRKEBARÁT

This most famous wine of the Badascony region is made from the French *Pinot Gris* grape. It is a full-bodied, sweet wine with a greenish gold color and fine fragrance. This rich wine is a good pairing with dessert.

KÉKNYELÜ

A delightful green golden wine with a full-bodied, powerful flavor.

ZOLDSZILVANI

This full-bodied yet pungent wine has a fine balanced taste and golden-greenish hue.

BALATON

The southern shore of Lake Balaton is the site of this wine region. Its rich and fertile soil, along with the advantageous reflections and heat-absorbing properties of the large water surface, allow this region to produce many quality wines.

BOGLÁRI MERLOT

A semi-sweet and full-bodied popular red wine that is made from a grape originating in France.

BOGLÁRI SAUVIGNON WHITE WINE

This wine is produced from the Sauvignon grape, originally from France. It has a subtle bouquet and aroma, with a freshness from its acidity.

TRAMINI

Originating from Austrian grapes, this elegant white wine has a spicy scent and aroma.

BALATONBOGLÁRI MUSKOTÁLY

This quality white wine is made from the Muscat Ottonel grape. It is light in character, with a soft and sweetish flavor and pleasant Muscat bouquet.

EGER

This is a beautiful baroque town in northeast Hungary, famous as the home of Bull's Blood (Egri Bikavér). The soil here is of soft volcanic rock—excellent red wine soil and easily carved to make the extensive underground cellars which are a chief feature of Eger. The wines of this region are aged for several years in oak barrels in these cellars.

BULL'S BLOOD (EGRI BIKAVÉR)

This full-flavored red wine is the most famous export wine of Hungary. The Kékfrankos grape variety, which yields a fine color and low acidity, is the chief component of this wine. Blended with other Cabernet, Blue Portuguese and Merlot grapes, the resulting wine is dark red, dry, silky and tangy.

The legend of the Bull's Blood (Egri Bikavér) dates from 1552, when the fortress of Eger, defended by the Hungarian hero István Dobó, was besieged by the overwhelming forces of the Turkish Army under Ali Pasha. The legend holds that the Hungarian men, strengthened by the quantities of Bull's Blood their women served them (the women were said to fight alongside the men in later stages of the siege), were able to withstand the Turkish onslaughts, and force the Ali Pasha to withdraw. The fortress of Egri remained unconquered thanks to the fortifying qualities of the Bull's Blood!

MÁTRAALJAI

The Mátraaljai district adjoins the Eger district on the foothills of the Mátra mountains. One of the biggest regions for quality white wines, the art of wine-making here dates back to the time of St. Stephen. The wines of this region range from elegant dry whites to sweet dessert wines.

DEBRÖI HÁRSLEVELÜ

This high quality wine is made from the Linden Leaf grape and is the best known wine of this region. It is a sweetish, aromatic wine of green-white color and a spicy aroma.

LÉANYKA

This popular white wine is made from an ancient grape nurtured by wine growers in this region for centuries. The wine is greenish-white in color, with a pleasant scent reminiscent of ripening grapes on the vine.

VILLÁNY-SIKLÓS

Villány-Siklós is famous as a red wine district. The abundant sunshine and high temperatures of this region produce grapes with substantial quantities of sugar. The Villány wines are well rounded, rich and full-bodied in taste.

VILLÁNYI KÉKFRANKOS

This deep red colored wine is made with a grape that originated in Austria. It is full bodied and fruity with a pleasant scent and pungent bouquet.

VILLÁNYI CABERNET SAUVIGNON

The Cabernet Sauvignon grape gives this dark ruby or deep red wine a noticeably fine spicy scent. This wine also has a pleasant tannic taste and richness.

SZEKSZÁRD

This south central Hungarian wine district has been renowned for its red wines since the days of the Romans in the fourth century. Its excellent full-bodied wines were said to be greatly favored by the Roman Emperors. The red wines of Szekszárd are generally in the Bordeaux style.

SZEKSZÁRDI VÖRÖS

This red Hungarian wine of strong character and harmonious composition, high in extract and best kept to mature, was one of several praised by Franz Liszt.

SZEKSZÁRDI BIKAVÉR

One of the most famous wines from the region, it is produced from the Kékfrankos, Kadarka and Cabernet grapes. This full-bodied, deep red wine has a spicy aroma and pleasant fragrance.

SOME RECOMMENDED PAIRINGS

TENDERLOIN STEAK AND OTHER BEEF DISHES

Villány Cabernet is a rich red wine, very pleasant and well balanced. Its flavor is dominated by prunes and mulberry, and its pleasant acidity comes the high tannin content of Villány wines. A good match with steaks and roasted beef.

Szekszárd Bull's Blood can compare with that from Eger, but it has a more mellow, less strong flavor. A dry, but rounded wine, with a characteristic sunny scent and flavor. Also works well paired with dessert.

FISH AND OTHER SEAFOOD

Etyek Sauvignon Blanc is an extra dry white wine that matches very well with fish, and is also recommended for marinating the fish. A faint straw-yellow color, intense flavor and long finish characterize this wine.

VENISON AND OTHER GAME

Cabernet Sauvignon from the Balaton is a strong red wine that unites the fruitiness of the grapes with rounded acidity and pleasant tannin. A good match with hearty stews, venison, duck and veal.

PORK

Tokay New Furmint is a light yellow colored wine with a subtle furmint grape taste. The wine has the pleasant flavors of bread crust, walnut and mushroom that come from the soil and climate. The superb balance of alcohol and acid makes this an excellent accompaniment to pork chops in a sweet sauce.

POULTRY AND VEGETARIAN DISHES

Italian Riesling from Halas is a light white wine with a golden yellow color and pleasant, pure Riesling scent. Its distinct flavor can balance out spicy stuffing and onions, making this wine an excellent pairing with fish, poultry and stuffed vegetable dishes.

DESSERTS

Badascony Szürkebarát, made from the *Pinot Gris* grape, is a full-bodied, sweet white wine. It has a gold-green color and delightful fragrance, making it a good match for sweets and desserts.

INDEX

INDEX

Hippocrene is NUMBER ONE in

International Cookbooks

Africa and Oceania
Best of Regional African Cooking
Good Food from Australia
Traditional South African Cookery

Asia and Near East
Best of Goan Cooking
The Joy of Chinese Cooking
The Art of South Indian Cooking
The Art of Persian Cooking
The Art of Israeli Cooking
The Art of Turkish Cooking

Mediterranean
Best of Greek Cuisine
Taste of Malta
A Spanish Family Cookbook

Western Europe
Art of Dutch Cooking
Best of Austrian Cuisine
A Belgian Cookbook
Celtic Cookbook
Traditional Recipes from Old England
The Art of Irish Cooking
Traditional Food from Scotland
Traditional Food from Wales

Scandinavia
Best of Scandinavian Cooking
The Best of Finnish Cooking
The Best of Smorgasbord Cooking
Good Food from Sweden

Central Europe
All Along the Danube
Bavarian Cooking
Bulgarian Cookbook
The Best of Czech Cooking
The Art of Hungarian Cooking
Polish Heritage Cookery
The Best of Polish Cooking
Old Warsaw Cookbook
Old Polish Traditions
Taste of Romania

Eastern Europe
The Cuisine of Armenia
The Best of Russian Cooking
The Best of Ukrainian Cuisine

Americas
Mayan Cooking
The Honey Cookbook
The Art of Brazilian Cookery
The Art of South American Cookery